DEVOTIONS®

December

⁓ Who in the skies above can compare with the
LORD?

— *Psalm 89:6*

Gary Wilde, Editor   **Margaret Williams,** Project Editor   Photo iStockphoto | Thinkstock®

DEVOTIONS® is published quarterly by Standard Publishing, Cincinnati, Ohio, www.standardpub.com.
© 2012 by Standard Publishing. All rights reserved. Topics based on the Home Daily Bible Readings,
International Sunday School Lessons. © 2010 by the Committee on the Uniform Series. Printed in
the U.S.A. All Scripture quotations, unless otherwise indicated, are taken from the *HOLY BIBLE,
NEW INTERNATIONAL VERSION®. NIV®.* Copyright © 1973, 1978, 1984, 2011 by Biblica, Inc.™.
Used by permission of Zondervan. All rights reserved. *King James Version (KJV),* public domain.

Obedience Doesn't Make Sense

"I am the Lord's servant," Mary answered. **"May your word to me be fulfilled." Then the angel left her** (Luke 1:38).

Scripture: Luke 1:26-40
Song: "Breath of Heaven"

My husband and I are in the midst of some financial struggles. For the first time in our lives, we don't always know how we're going to pay all our bills, and we're living paycheck to paycheck. Nevertheless, we feel convinced that God wants us to bless others with what little we have. So we've decided to tithe anyway, even though the numbers don't add up. Through it all, we're learning to trust that God will provide, and so far He hasn't failed us.

When the angel told Mary she would give birth to Jesus, she replied, "How will this be . . . since I am a virgin?"(v. 34). The angel's announcement that Mary would carry God's Son into the world didn't make sense to her, but she still agreed to follow God's plans.

Is God asking you to do something that doesn't make sense to you? Consider the story of Mary. God asked her to help bring His Son into the world. She obeyed, and the whole world was blessed.

Thank You, **Lord**, for Mary's example of faith and obedience. Thank You for sending Your Son to our world. Today I will face problems that seem to have no solutions, and I will need Your guidance in order to move forward in faith. Please help me to be obedient to You, even when it doesn't make sense. Through Christ I pray. Amen.

December 1–7. **Andrea Osmun** is a freelance writer from Cleveland, Ohio, who finds her inspiration to write flowing from her loving Savior and from her precious family.

He's the Source

The LORD sends poverty and wealth; he humbles and he exalts (1 Samuel 2:7).

Scripture: 1 Samuel 2:1-10
Song: "Blessed Be the Name"

When I was a kid, I always thought that if I worked hard enough, I would have everything I needed in life: money, a good job, a house, cars. Basically, I thought I could live comfortably. Life doesn't come together that easily, though.

I survived two layoffs and left a company just before it went bankrupt. I kept wondering why God would allow that to happen to me, since I had always worked so hard. However, as I've been learning lately, possessions and financial security are only temporary. The security that comes from God is eternal.

In the Bible, Hannah had a wonderful dream, a deep desire, but it was withheld from her for awhile: She couldn't bear children. And to make matters worse, her husband's other wife was taunting her because of it. She cried out to God in the temple, and He listened. He gave her a baby boy, Samuel, and she dedicated him to God. In her dedication prayer, instead of focusing on the amazing gift she had received, Hannah acknowledged the gift-giver.

Isn't that what God wants from us, as well? To acknowledge Him as the source of everything we have and everything we need? Whether He gives us a little or a lot, every good thing comes from His hand.

Dear God, thank You for meeting all of my needs—and for every good thing You give me. I acknowledge You as the source of everything I have. In Jesus' name, amen.

Just Try It!

Taste and see that the LORD is good; blessed is the one who takes refuge in him (Psalm 34:8)

Scripture: Psalm 34:1-8
Song: "Taste and See"

My husband, Keith, is the pickiest eater I know. He could eat peanut butter and jelly sandwiches for lunch every day of the week and be happy. The only vegetables he'll eat are green beans and corn; he hates berries of all kinds, and he doesn't like creams or sauces.

Being from a Croatian family, I'm used to trying all kinds of new foods. Sometimes I'll come across a food that tastes so delicious, I just have to convince Keith to try it. Often he's reluctant, but I've been able to persuade him.

In today's Scripture, David seems to be saying about God what I've been saying to my husband all this time about food: "Just try it. I know you'll like it."

David, the psalm writer, was in a tough situation, harassed and pursued by a murderous king. Yet David encouraged God's people to rejoice in the Lord and trust in Him, because God answers prayer and delivers His beloved ones from trouble. From personal experience, David could say: "God is good" (Psalm 73:1).

When you're not sure of God's goodness in your troubles, just "taste and see" (v. 8) what it means to enjoy fellowship with Him throughout each day. You won't be disappointed.

Dear Lord, thank You for David's example in tough times. When I doubt Your goodness in my life, please help me to turn to You, trusting that You will come through for me, in Your way and in Your time. In Jesus' name, amen.

Joy Through Thanksgiving

Enter his gates with thanksgiving and his courts with praise; give thanks to him and praise his name (Psalm 100:4).

Scripture: Psalm 100
Song: "Give to Our God Immortal Praise"

In the past two weeks, my husband has lost his job, we lost our family health insurance, our car broke down, and a family member was diagnosed with cancer. Yet somehow, we are finding joy in being grateful for the blessings God has poured into our lives down through the years.

Of course, it's so easy to focus on the negatives! But when we do, we end up feeling depressed and arguing with each other. So, Keith and I have determined to focus on the goodness of God, knowing He's in complete control of our circumstances.

One of my favorite Bible passages is Philippians 4:6, 7, which says, "Do not be anxious about anything, but in every situation, by prayer and petition, with thanksgiving, present your requests to God. And the peace of God, which transcends all understanding, will guard your hearts and your minds in Christ Jesus."

When we come before God with thanksgiving and praise, focusing on His goodness instead of our troubles, we walk away with a supernatural peace. We're not sure what the future holds, but we do know that God is good. Therefore, we have reason to thank and praise Him each new day.

Dear Father, thank You for all the good things You give me and my family. Even when we struggle through difficult times, we know that You are in control. I thank You and praise You today, through Christ my Lord. Amen.

God the Loving Father

As a father has compassion on his children, so the LORD has compassion on those who fear him (Psalm 103:13).

Scripture: Psalm 103:13-22
Song: "Children of God"

Television these days doesn't offer many examples of good fathering, does it? Just turn on the TV, and you'll soon come across a dad who's fairly irresponsible in his approach to his family—and life in general. He's often portrayed as drinking, chasing after women, and spending his evenings on the couch immersed in sports.

Some of us can relate to these portrayals, because our own fathers are (or were), in fact, like this. Others of us grew up with good fathers who paid loving attention to us and conveyed a godly example to follow. This is important, because our "God image" is significantly shaped by our experience of earthly fatherhood. Even though we know what the Scriptures say about our heavenly Father's character, we can't deny the impact of our biological dad, for good or ill.

In any case, let us familiarize ourselves with what God says about His character in Scripture. Thus we can bring into focus the beautiful portrait of Him as the loving Father He is. He's certainly not the lackadaisical dad of television notoriety. He is never abusive and harsh toward us. He doesn't crush us with His power. Instead, He treats us with compassion and love, despite our frail, broken condition.

Dear Heavenly Father, thank You for Your compassionate fatherhood. Today I praise You for Your loving care in my life. In the name of Jesus, amen.

Legacy of Love: A Way of Life

The fear of the LORD is the beginning of wisdom; all who follow his precepts have good understanding. To him belongs eternal praise (Psalm 111:10).

Scripture: Psalm 111
Song: "Children of the World"

Every night, as part of my daughter's bedtime routine, I sing "Jesus, Jesus, Lord to Me" in remembrance of my grandmother, who sang it to me when I was little. My grandma lived with my family from when I was 11 years old until I was about 16. Every day, she woke up at sunrise and read her Bible. At night, she'd tuck my brother and me into our beds and sing us that lovely song.

In Psalm 111, David praised the Lord in front of other believers, recounting the many ways God had been faithful to them. He encouraged his people to fear God and obey His Word, because God was worthy of their reverence, obedience, and praise. David passed down to his son Solomon this "fear of the Lord," he repeated it throughout the book of Proverbs.

My grandmother didn't just pass a song down to me, a tune and some lyrics. No, she handed me *a way of life*, a life filled with praise for all the Lord is to us. I want to pass my grandmother's legacy of love to my own daughter. I want her to remember all the great works of our heavenly Father and pass the good news of His love to future generations.

Dear God, You are worthy of our praise because You have been faithful to us for generations. May I hand Your legacy of love on to my children and their children. In Jesus' name I pray. Amen.

Change We Can Believe In

Do not put your trust in princes, in human beings, who cannot save (Psalm 146:3).

Scripture: Psalm 146
Song: "Trust in Jesus"

Every year we have elections, whether for local, state, or federal government positions. And every year we watch as candidates make promises they can't keep. We do our best to vote with the knowledge available to us, hoping that our candidate of choice will take office and then make the changes we desire.

But we should always ask ourselves: *How much are we trusting others to fix our problems?*

The psalmist reminds us that, ultimately, only God can deliver us. He champions our cause, knows all of our struggles, sets us free from the chains of sin, and provides for our needs. What politician can do that?

We Christians should vote, of course, because it is our right as American citizens, and we can thereby help influence society for the good. Nevertheless, we do well to remember that the promises of politicians are many . . . and fleeting. As one anonymous quipster put it: "To succeed in politics, it is often necessary to rise above your principles." Haven't we often seen it?

Promises from God aren't empty, though. They're eternal and flow from His holy character. So let us put our hope and trust in the only one who can make a lasting difference.

Dear God, thank You for championing our cause, for seeing our struggles, and providing for our needs. I claim You as my deliverer today, putting all my trust in You. In the name of the Father and of the Son and of the Holy Spirit, amen.

Let Us Glorify Him!

My soul doth magnify the Lord, and my spirit hath rejoiced in God my Saviour (Luke 1:46, *King James Version*).

Scripture: Luke 1:46-56
Song: "Mary's Boy Child"

Our Scripture today is known to Christians around the world as the Magnificat. The word comes from the first line in the Latin text: *Magnificat anima mea Dominum* ("My soul doth magnify the Lord"). *Magnificat*, then, is translated "magnify" or "glorify."

So what does it mean to *glorify* the Lord? In the original biblical languages, it conveys the idea of weightiness. For instance, we might say of someone that he's a "heavyweight" of a personality, or a "substantial" personage. We're not talking about weight in pounds; we're referring to a significance of character.

Thus to glorify God is to recognize, proclaim, and honor His weighty personhood, His heavy majesty, His substantial holiness. Jehovah is no small deity who created the cosmos, no "lightweight" who flung the stars into the universe.

Mary knew all this and proclaimed it. Even more, she acknowledged a heavenly mercy: the king of the universe bending down to her in order to use her mightily in the plan of salvation. Mary would bear the Messiah; she knew she was blessed.

Can we too think of good reasons to lift up a magnificat today? Has God blessed us, been merciful, shown us His mighty deeds, and filled us with good things? Let us glorify His name.

Father, I glorify You today for all the goodness and mercy You have poured into my life. Thank You, in Jesus' name. Amen.

December 8. **Gary Wilde** is a minister and freelance writer who lives in Bonita Springs, Florida.

Obedient Servant

Everyone who heard this wondered about it, asking, "What then is this child going to be? For the Lord's hand was with him" (Luke 1:66).

Scripture: Luke 1:59-66
Song: "O How Happy Are They Who the Savior Obey"

My father-in-law has trusted the Lord all of his life. He grew up poor, worked hard, earned five academic degrees, and had a distinguished career. The Lord blessed him with love, generosity, and a desire to help others.

For as long as I can remember, he has visited and encouraged people in hospitals and nursing homes. He has been an elder of his church for over 40 years and shared his professional expertise with family and friends. They all say the same thing: "I wish I could be like him." His passionate prayers have touched the hearts of listeners for years. So many lives have been transformed because he bowed to the Lord's will.

When we obey Him, the Lord's hand is with us. If Elizabeth and Zechariah hadn't obeyed God all of their lives, John the Baptist might never have been born to this once barren couple. And without John, who would have spread the word about the coming Messiah? It seems that obedience plays a large role in releasing God's activity in the world.

Father, thank You for the people in my life who serve as marvelous examples of Your love. Help me follow Your commands as I emulate those who went before me in faith and obedience. In all things, may I bring glory to Your name, through Christ. Amen.

December 9–15. **Nancy Dutton** is a freelance writer who lives in the Rocky Mountains of Colorado. She helps the elderly, loves her family and friends, and greatly enjoys the outdoors.

Baptized Together

He went into all the country around the Jordan, preaching a baptism of repentance for the forgiveness of sins (Luke 3:3).

Scripture: Luke 3:1-6
Song: "Shall We Gather at the River?"

At Christmas time, as lights glowed on the pine trees in the church sanctuary, my husband and I walked to the front and then stepped down into warm water to be baptized. The minister dipped me into the water first. I gladly surrendered myself in faith to the Lord. I already knew my previous lifestyle no longer worked for me: The stress of devoting all of my time to career and money had brought me illness and low energy.

When the minister submerged my husband, joy filled my soul, knowing we would share this new life in Christ together in the coming years. I never wanted that smile on my face to disappear. What a relief it was to let go of the past, accept God's forgiveness, and look forward to our exciting future as a team guided by Jesus, now and through eternity.

Yes, our baptism was a refreshing act of repentance—and dedication to the Lord. Now, incorporated into the body of Christ, we would seek to do His will each day.

Have you taken the plunge in His living water of spiritual life? Without Jesus, we would be drowning, with no hope. No wonder the preaching of John was so powerful!

O Merciful Father, the opportunity to repent and to be forgiven changed my life. I rejoice and thank You, God, for washing away my sins. Help me, each day, to seek Your will and follow Your ways. In the precious name of Jesus, amen.

What Could I Share?

John answered, "Anyone who has two shirts should share with the one who has none, and anyone who has food should do the same" (Luke 3:11).

Scripture: Luke 3:7-14
Song: "Lord, Thou Lov'st the Cheerful Giver"

God calls us to produce fruit by giving what we have. My friend Shirley is retired, living on a fixed income, but always eager to give to others. She lifts people's spirits wherever she goes. She sings for them, says an encouraging word, and compliments them. God has taught me much about giving through observing Shirley's way of life.

Once a month Shirley cleans and organizes her closet. She washes clothes she no longer wears and gives me her new-looking outfits. I give the ones that don't fit to the less fortunate and pass on the joy. Thus Shirley's sharing multiplies the blessings.

At her house, Shirley offers me chocolate cake and iced tea. When a church member grieves for a loved one, she takes them food for dinner. A smile, a kind word doesn't cost anything to give. When Shirley and I go shopping, she tells the saleslady about Jesus. Our next destination is usually a restaurant. When a waitress told us about a physical problem, Shirley put her hands on the woman and prayed. Tears streamed down the woman's face, and her eyes lit up with hope.

This Christmas season, could we help someone with Christlike kindness? I'm thinking right now: What could I share?

Dear Father, You gave Your only Son to die for me. Please grant me a giving heart to share what I have. In Jesus' precious name I pray. Amen.

Cleansing Agent

John answered them all, "I baptize you with water. But one who is more powerful than I will come, the straps of whose sandals I am not worthy to untie. He will baptize you with the Holy Spirit and fire" (Luke 3:16).

Scripture: Luke 3:15-20
Song: "Holy Spirit, Truth Divine"

As my husband rode his bicycle around the lake near our house, he came to a small bridge over a gully. Up ahead he saw the grass below a cottonwood tree burst into flames. It happened so fast, it was as if someone threw a torch on that grass.

Firemen responded quickly, dousing out the blaze, but that parcel of grass—and half of the tree—were black. A few months later, though, the grass grew back greener than ever. A red-twig dogwood bush sprang up where one had never grown before. The fire cleansed the land and prepared it for new growth.

John was God's appointed messenger who prepared the way for Jesus. John baptized with water, a symbol of cleansing away sin. Jesus baptized with the Holy Spirit and fire. When we're baptized, God puts His Spirit into us. Through the Holy Spirit, we know the power of God, which is demonstrated in the resurrection of Jesus. The "fire" is the presence of the Holy Spirit, who acts as a cleansing agent, burning up what is not good in us—as we allow Him to do so. He purifies and prepares us for our life with the holy trinity in Heaven.

Almighty and gracious Father, I am grateful for being born anew, so I may live with You in Your kingdom forever. May I this day be "on fire" with the Holy Spirit. O Lord, cleanse and prepare me for new growth! In Jesus' name, amen.

I'm His Child Too

A voice from heaven said, "This is my Son, whom I love; with him I am well pleased" (Matthew 3:17).

Scripture: Matthew 3:13-17
Song: "The Family of God"

We enjoy a family reunion every Fourth of July in the woods near a lake and a river. The women arrange all of the homemade food, keep everyone fed, brew the coffee, and oversee the children (who have ongoing watermelon fights). The men barbecue meat while telling stories and flying remote-controlled aircraft. Another relative shows the old home movies. We treasure this time together as we catch up on our lives, connecting to our heritage and enjoying the companionship of our loved ones.

"When you believed," says Ephesians 1:13, 14, "you were marked in him with a seal, the promised Holy Spirit, who is a deposit guaranteeing our inheritance until the redemption of those who are God's possession."

In other words, when we receive the Holy Spirit in baptism, we become adopted children of God, full members of His family. After Jesus was baptized, the voice from Heaven identified Him as the Son of God, and—in Him—we too are now God's children, brothers and sisters in Christ, coheirs to His heavenly throne through eternity.

Today, I will remember that voice from Heaven, for it still speaks. I will listen for it when I have a chance to stop and recollect who I really am: a beloved daughter of the king.

O Loving Father, I am humbly honored to be a part of Your family. Thank You for sending the Holy Spirit to direct me in Your ways. In Jesus' name I pray. Amen.

Jesus, Our Healer

At that very time Jesus cured many who had diseases, sicknesses and evil spirits, and gave sight to many who were blind (Luke 7:21).

Scripture: Luke 7:18-27
Song: "Jesus Heals"

Gravely ill, I was afraid of dying as I suffered from severe and painful digestive issues that left me barely able to eat and swallow food. All I could do was lie in bed and sit up briefly. I prayed and then read Luke 7:21. Jesus healed many people plagued with diseases and illnesses. Why wouldn't He heal me too? Even if I didn't get completely well, any improvement would be an encouragement.

Every morning and evening I listened to a CD of Scriptures about healing. My faith that Jesus would renew my health increased. I read the Bible daily and started a prayer list. Praying for other people helped them, and it brought me closer to God. My hope grew.

And God started reviving my body. When I could sit up longer, I wrote poetry and short stories. A nutritionist guided me as to what foods to eat. Soon I could drive and shop at the grocery store half a mile away. I attended a weekly Bible study where others prayed over me, and the Word of God energized me. My digestive problems diminished. Jesus brought me from the brink of death to restored health.

Great Physician, I praise You for soothing my physical ailments. Most of all, thank You for granting me new life. I joyously look forward to the time we will be together in the new earth, where death and sickness no longer exist. Through Christ, amen.

Praise the Lord

Zechariah was filled with the Holy Spirit and prophesied: Praise be to the Lord, the God of Israel, because he has come to his people and redeemed them (Luke 1:67, 68).

Scripture: Luke 1:57, 58, 67-79
Song: "O for a Thousand Tongues to Sing"

The word *praise* appears in more than 300 verses of the Bible. The dictionary says *praise* means to worship, glorify, value, merit, commend, express a favorable judgment of. In Zechariah's song, the priest and prophet overflowed with thanks for the birth of his son, John the Baptist. He also gave thanks for the rescuing of his people.

Praising the Lord can transform your ho-hum or difficult day into a joyful experience. When the Holy Spirit came to live inside me, my eyes opened to how the Lord wanted me to live. Actions and omissions of a lifetime played through my head. A myriad of emotions raced in my heart. I felt deep sorrow for people I had hurt, forgiveness for those who'd hurt me, and happiness for the promise of eternal life. I exalted the Lord for delivering me from such an unsatisfying life.

Now whenever I feel grumpy, fearful, or overwhelmed, I glorify Him with grateful praises. Are you experiencing difficulties? Sing aloud praises to Him, feel His love for you, and rejoice in the hope that flows from His mercy.

Dear Father in Heaven, I praise You for waking me up to Your love and saving my soul, so I am free to enjoy each day in peace with Your love. Give me a spirit of gratitude amidst all the joys and sorrows of this life, until I enter the next life! In the name of Jesus, my Lord and Savior, amen.

Make Good Your Word

So now I give him to the LORD. For his whole life he will be given over to the LORD (1 Samuel 1:28).

Scripture: 1 Samuel 1:21-28
Song: "We Are an Offering"

"God, if you'll just let me make this putt, then I'll . . ." "God, if you'll just let us buy this house . . ." "God, if you'll just deliver me from this . . ." Have you ever bargained with God like that? Maybe it wasn't on the golf course or at the realtor's office. Maybe it was something far more serious, like the health of your child or the pending death of someone close. I think we've all at least *thought* about it, even if we haven't actually spoken the words. But when the deal has been struck, how many of us have kept our end of the bargain?

I'm intrigued by Elkanah's response in today's Scripture. He said in verse 23, "[Only may] the Lord make good his word." I'm not sure what he meant by this, but I chuckle to think that Elkanah was in some way questioning God's integrity. After all, when was the last time God failed to keep a promise?

I think the more pressing question is whether or not we'll make good *our* word. Hannah was true. She kept up her end of the deal and dedicated Samuel to the Lord. That's got to be our goal. May we always be faithful like Hannah. May we always be true to our word.

Lord, I pray that You'll be honored with my life. Strengthen me to keep every promise I've ever made to You, or before You. In Jesus' name I pray. Amen.

December 16–22. **Von Mitchell** is a high school teacher and basketball coach in Delta, Colorado. Married for 19 years to Marcia, the love of his life, he is also a big In-N-Out Burger fan.

The Power of a Smile

The LORD make his face shine upon you and be gracious to you (Numbers 6:25).

Scripture: Numbers 6:22-27
Song: "Revive Us Again"

It really is a universal statement. Smiles translate into every possible language and dialect under the sun. Smiles are a good thing, and we all know it. Smiles brighten up the world. I love smiles.

As a public high school teacher, I know that sometimes the students in my classroom are having a bad day. If I can get them to smile, everyone's day gets a little better. Many of my students' parents speak little or no English. But they understand it when I smile at them during parent/teacher conferences, and I understand it when they smile back at me. Smiles help create understanding. Smiles convey goodwill. Smiles help us bridge the communication gap.

Who wouldn't want a smile from God? If we thought that His face was shining upon us, wouldn't that be similar to a smile?

I don't know about you, but I'd travel many miles just to get a smile from the Creator. In my own life, I'm working out "with fear and trembling" (see Philippians 2:12, 13) just how much of that smile I will enjoy some day. But make no mistake, I long for God's face to shine upon me. How about you?

O God, Creator of Heaven and earth, I pray that Your face would shine upon me. And may my life be the best smile I can produce for Your glory. I pray this prayer in the name of Jesus, my merciful Savior and Lord. Amen.

The Great Light

The people walking in darkness have seen a great light; on those living in the land of deep darkness a light has dawned (Isaiah 9:2).

Scripture: Isaiah 9:1-5
Song: "Something Changed"

I once had to drive from Eureka Springs, Arkansas, to Cedaredge, Colorado, in one day, by myself. It's about an 18-hour trip. As you can imagine, I left quite early in the morning while it was still dark.

I was so sleepy! I couldn't wait for the sun to come out and wake up the day. Somewhere on the highway in the great state of Oklahoma, between turtles and tollbooths, a light dawned and dispelled my drowsy darkness. I felt much better (until "turnpike trance" settled in somewhere around Kansas). After that, I was on a beeline to get home.

How many times has your life felt like an isolated 18-hour road trip in the darkness—without a map? Even if you've walked with Christ for some time, you undoubtedly have still experienced difficult days. We all do. But the good news trumpeted in the book of Isaiah is for all of us. The Light has come!

Like merry sunshine on our souls is the dawning of Christ as Lord in our hearts. Even in the darkest hours of our lives, Jesus will light the way and ignite us with passion and purpose—until, eventually, we all make it home.

O Eternal Lord God, thank You for lighting my way and igniting my heart with a fire to serve you. May you be glorified in my life through the things I do and say, and think. This is my prayer, in the name of Jesus. Amen.

Pointing to Him

But you, Bethlehem Ephrathah, though you are small among the clans of Judah, out of you will come for me one who will be ruler over Israel. . . . And he will be our peace (Micah 5:2, 5).

Scripture: Micah 5:1-5
Song: "Peace, Peace, Wonderful Peace"

I have a friend who sees God's story in almost everything. If a runner falls down at a track meet—my friend the Father who picks us up when we fall. A falsely accused man spends 20 years of his life in prison—my friend sees the chance to forgive as Jesus did. A kid on the brink of suicide until a sports icon takes him to dinner—my friend sees *hope*. My friend's capacity to see all of life's events pointing to the Lord amazes me. But so does the Bible—for the written Word constantly points us to the *living word*.

I am amazed to know that the five verses in today's Scripture point to Jesus. This passage was written nearly 700 years before Jesus came to earth.

It seems the entire Bible is a tapestry with a constant thread: *Jesus*. It's a screenplay with a consistent theme: *for God so loved the world* (John 3:16). It's an essay with a life-changing thesis: *We exist to glorify Him*.

Will you be ready to see God's story in your circumstances today? No matter what you have scheduled, take a moment to see the hand of God in your life.

Dear God, I pray that all of my life would point to you—not to me, O Lord, or to anything else. Give me the peace that comes in knowing that all things are in Your sovereign hands. Through Christ, amen.

~ Victory! ~

You exalted me above my foes; from a violent man you rescued me. Therefore I will praise you, LORD, among the nations; I will sing the praises of your name (Psalm 18:48, 49).

Scripture: Psalm 18:46-50
Song: "Victory in Jesus"

Old-school Denver Broncos fans aren't likely to ever forget Super Bowl XXXII. That was the day the Broncos won their first Super Bowl over the heavily favored Green Bay Packers. It was a special day made even sweeter because Denver had suffered lopsided defeats on the big stage so many times before—first to the Cowboys back in 1978 (I cried my 8-year-old self to sleep that night), then to the Giants, Redskins, and 49ers in later years. But only tears of joy were flowing after Super Bowl XXXII. The reason? V-I-C-T-O-R-Y!

We all lose sometimes. No one goes undefeated through this life. And sometimes we even lose to the same opponent, over and over again.

But victory is in store for the upright (see Proverbs 2:7). As believers, we have a common foe who seeks to steal, kill, and destroy us (John 10:10). Yet think of how many victories God has marshaled despite the opposition—and those in a conflict much more important than football.

So, like my beloved Broncos, let's keep striving. Let's be strong in God's mighty power (Ephesians 6:10) and give Him praise for all the victories in our lives!

Lord, thank You for victory over an enemy who seeks to destroy me in any way possible. I praise You that You have exalted me above my foes. In Jesus' name, amen.

Really? Wow!

So you are no longer a slave, but God's child; and since you are his child, God has made you also an heir (Galatians 4:7).

Scripture: Galatians 4:1-7
Song: "Martyrs and Thieves"

Not too long ago, my wife and I watched the movie *Little Giants* starring actor Rick Moranis. There's a scene in the film where they hand the football to a little, timid kid whose dad is coming for the first time to see his son play.

Dad stands at the far goalpost, so the little boy weaves in and out of defenders as he runs. Those tacklers are trying to annihilate him en route to the end zone—and his father's arms. It's a telling scene about the love between a father and son. Both of us got a little misty.

Fast forward now to the father-child dynamic in your relationship with God. I don't know about you, but I struggle to grasp this concept: I am God's beloved child.

With my finite mind I try, but I fall short. *Are you serious, Lord? Really? Me, a son? You'd be waiting for me in the end zone?* It boggles my mind every time I think of it. But this biblical pronouncement has led me to one of the best conclusions I've made as an adult: God is not limited by my understanding. In fact, He's not limited by anything about me. Only I am.

So that settles it. God said it. I believe it. I'm not just a son. I'm an heir. Wow!

O gracious God, thank You for Your Word. Thank You for truth. I pray for insight and I cry out for understanding—to grasp what You have said about my adopted sonship. May I remember this great fact every day of my life. In Jesus' name, amen.

It Happened!

Today in the town of David a Savior has been born to you; he is the Messiah, the Lord (Luke 2:11).

Scripture: Luke 2:1-17
Song: "Joy to the World!"

My mother was born on Christmas Day in 1940. Before my grandma passed away, she used to tell me about that day. "Have you ever just wanted something so bad?" she'd ask. "Well, that's how it was when your mother was born. I wanted her with all I was worth. And then it happened. I got her. I got the best present in the whole world!"

I was always quick to agree. My mother is a present. She's the one who holds us all together. She's worth celebrating, every day of the year.

Close to 2,000 years before my mom entered the world, the person that all prophecy had been pointing to was born. It finally happened. And what a gift He was! To think that He split history into BC and AD—and that we still celebrate His birthday today. Talk about the best present.

Gram told me the story more than once of Mom being born and I never got tired of it. I've read or heard the Christmas story hundreds of times, but I never tire of it. That's the thing about great stories—they never get old. Jesus came down and made His home among us. He took on flesh and lived a sinless life on our behalf. Praise God. It happened!

O God, the king of glory, I praise You today for all you have done. Thank You for unwrapping the best present in our hearts and showing us how to live out the life He has put within us. Through this same Christ, my Lord and Savior, I pray. Amen.

This Baby Belongs to God!

Joseph and Mary took him to Jerusalem to present him to the Lord (as it is written in the Law of the Lord, "Every firstborn male is to be consecrated to the Lord") (Luke 2:22, 23).

Scripture: Luke 2:21-24
Song: "Silent Night"

Alone in my hospital bed, I held my first baby in my arms. No one else was in the room. A serene sense of holiness and peace seemed to surround my newborn son and me in the stillness of the night. It happened to be close to Christmas, which gave me a fresh new bond with Mary, thinking how the mother of my Lord must have felt holding baby Jesus.

What a miracle to hold my new baby and to consider this fact: though he was born from me, I did not make him or own him. Nor could I protect him from all the harsh things that come with simply being a human in this world.

Yet he had come through me and was put in my care for a season of time. It would be my job to nurture and raise him to know and love God who sent him. I knew I couldn't give my son all he needed on my own. I asked God to help me raise this child (who was really His.) Holding my newborn son before the Lord, I asked that my precious baby's life be blessed and set apart so that others might know he belonged to the Lord.

Father, it is impossible to know what You felt as You sent Jesus to be born as one of us in the form of a helpless baby. But thank You for giving Him! In His name, amen.

December 23–29. **Eva Juliuson,** who writes from Oklahoma City, Oklahoma, loves to see others grow deeper in the Lord through prayer.

The Only True Cleaner

How much more, then, will the blood of Christ, who through the eternal Spirit offered himself unblemished to God, cleanse our consciences from acts that lead to death, so that we may serve the living God! (Hebrews 9:14).

Scripture: Leviticus 12:1-5
Song: "Blood of His Covenant"

Cleaning the church I grew up in was an act of love for me. This particular night seemed even more special, since the next day would be a Christmas service. I vacuumed between the pews and prayed for those who regularly sat there. I recalled my baptism, my marriage, my children's baptisms, my husband's and my dad's funerals, and my kids' marriages; they were all held in that little church. I worked extra hard so the church would look sparkling clean for the service and for my whole church family.

The ladies' bathroom was the last place to clean. Everything had a fresh look . . . except for one stubborn brown stain in the sink. I had used some strong cleanser on it, but it just wouldn't come out. (I did know of a cleaner that would wipe out that stain, but I didn't have any.) Surely no one would notice; the rest of the church was so immaculate.)

You guessed it! The next day a lady pointed out that brown spot on the sink. Because it was Christmas, I was reminded that no matter how hard we try to look good, there is only one who can truly cleanse the stains of our sin.

Father, thank You for Jesus, who was born in a manger and willingly sacrificed himself for me. Thank You for His precious blood, the only solution to eternally cleanse our dark stain of sin. Through His holy name I pray. Amen.

Gift of Life!

Just as the Son of Man did not come to be served, but to serve, and to give His life as a ransom for many (Matthew 20:28).

Scripture: Leviticus 12:6-8
Song: "When I Survey the Wondrous Cross"

My neighbor had been on the heart transplant list for many years. Charles had far outlived the few years the doctors had predicted when he was still in his twenties. Though his life had been lived in and out of the hospital, he still had been able to raise his daughters and enjoy being a grandpa. But then a phone call came about a heart that was finally available.

After all those years of struggling for breath and energy and fighting huge battles for his very life, he received the heart of a 19-year-old young man who'd died in a motorcycle accident. Not only did Charles get a new lease on life, but so did four other people who received the young man's liver, kidney, eyes, and lungs.

My neighbor told me about the emotional meeting when the young man's parents met each of those who received new life through their son's organs. These parents never dreamed, when they held their newborn son, that someday he would lose his life and others would live.

Yet our heavenly Father knew all along His Son would take our death so we could have eternal life. We should be offering gifts to our king; instead, He made himself a sacrifice for us.

Heavenly Father, what an amazing gift! You gave Your own Son to be sacrificed so I could live. There is no greater gift, and I thank You! Through Christ, amen.

Tender Judgment

Speak tenderly to Jerusalem, and proclaim to her that her hard service has been completed, that her sin has been paid for, that she has received from the LORD's hand double for all her sins (Isaiah 40:2).

Scripture: Isaiah 40:1-5
Song: "Amazing Grace"

My husband and I waited with dread outside the court-room. We were guilty, and we knew it. We had borrowed money against land homesteaded by family to start a business. It seemed like a good idea at the time. In order to keep the business going, we ran up bills and had to borrow more money.

We worked long hours, desperate for the business to work. Our funding plans kept getting more complicated until we realized there was no way out of our mess. We needed to admit our guilt and declare our inability to pay our debts before a judge.

When we appeared before the judge, we held our heads in shame as creditors listed the debts we owed. As the judge looked at our list of assets (or lack of them) and the remorse we felt, he told our creditors to be quiet. He raised the gavel and declared us free of all the financial burdens that had held us prisoner for so long. With a kind look, he told us to go and make a new life.

This was such a marvelous picture of God's tender mercy in my life. All my unbearable sins were gone, and in their place was a fresh new start.

Holy Father! Thank You for open eyes to see my sin and guilt. Thank You for Jesus who has taken my shame and given me new life. In His name, I pray. Amen.

God's Wristwatch

This is what the LORD says: "In the time of my favor I will answer you, and in the day of salvation I will help you" (Isaiah 49:8).

Scripture: Isaiah 49:8-13
Song: "They That Wait Upon the Lord"

"I'm going to give God a wristwatch," my friend joked, "so He'll realize when it's time to help me!" She was known for complaining that God ran late a little too often. Don't we all feel like that at times—because we want God to synchronize His watch with ours? We think we know the right moment for things to happen. Yet God calls us to trust Him and His promises, even when we don't see much happening.

The Jewish people had been waiting for a promised Messiah forever. And they had their ideas about exactly *how* this Savior would save them. Most of them apparently believed He would release them from Roman rule. Yet all along, God had His perfect plan, one that far surpassed human comprehension. He sent Jesus at just the right time to offer eternal salvation.

When we willingly enter the waters of baptism, we can also accept God's timing for the rest of our lives. Then, whatever the circumstances are, we can take joy in knowing that God has deep compassion for us and travels the road with us. Our Lord wants the very best for us and is at work in our lives. When we trust Him, we can willingly synchronize our timing with His.

Eternal God, You look far beyond the concept of time as we know it. Thank You for guiding my life with infinite wisdom and unfailing compassion. I pray this prayer in the name of Jesus, my Savior and Lord. Amen.

Servant . . . Son . . . King!

Here is my servant, whom I uphold, my chosen one in whom I delight; I will put my Spirit on him, and he will bring justice to the nations (Isaiah 42:1).

Scripture: Isaiah 42:1-7
Song: "Above All"

It takes a lot of courage to run for president in our country. Another candidate's full-time staff is working to dig up dirt on you! They will surely find something on a presidential hopeful, for there is no such thing as a perfect candidate.

In fact, the Bible says that everyone has sinned and fallen short of the glory of God. All except for one! Jesus, pure and unblemished, lived the perfect life for us, fulfilling the commandments to the letter. As our high priest, He also offered the perfect sacrifice—both priest and victim—to completely atone for our sin.

Jesus, the second person of the Trinity, God Almighty, doesn't need our vote. He was already sovereign before He ever accepted the Father's request to humble himself as a servant to be born as one of us. Our king was sent to live life amidst the same human challenges we face daily. Only He never failed to do the right thing.

No one but Jesus was worthy to save us. No one but Jesus served so unselfishly. No one but Jesus reigns forevermore at the right hand of God. No one but Jesus deserves to be our king.

Father, how can we ever thank You for the gift of Your Son, Jesus? He reigns above all, yet lowered himself to be our servant. Thanks to You, in Jesus' name. Amen.

The Answer: Bundled in Blankets

Now there was a man in Jerusalem called Simeon, who was righteous and devout. He was waiting for the consolation of Israel, and the Holy Spirit was on him (Luke 2:25).

Scripture: Luke 2:25-38
Song: "Open the Eyes of My Heart, Lord"

Once a month, I invite all my grandchildren over for "Grandkids Night." We always hold hands around the table and pray before eating. More than once, when we are finished praying, one of them will say, "Mamaw! They had their eyes open!" I laugh and remind them that they wouldn't know unless their own eyes were open. Then I try to explain that there are times it's OK to pray with your eyes open (like when you're driving or walking outside).

Simeon and Anna had both been praying for many years with their eyes wide open. Scripture doesn't tell us if they kept their physical eyes open, but they had been waiting and watching for many years. They had dedicated their lives to watching to see when God would send His promised Messiah.

I don't know if they ever grew discouraged or thought about giving up. One thing I do know is this: They immediately recognized Jesus when Joseph and Mary brought Him to the temple. They saw the answer to all their prayers bundled in blankets. Maybe we should practice keeping our eyes open every time we pray—to see how God will lead us *this* time.

Gracious Father, as I bring my requests to You in prayer, help me watch for all the creative ways You will answer and lead. Remind me to watch and pray at all times! Thank You, in Jesus' name. Amen.

Mercy Incarnate

Wilt thou be made whole? (John 5:6, *King James Version*).

Scripture: John 5:2-17
Song: "Beside the Gospel Pool"

On cots and crutches, the blind, halt, and lame crowded the porches surrounding the healing pool. Each person hoped he'd be the first into the pool, when the water was stirred (v. 7) so that healing might follow.

For some, this was the first try; for others, perhaps the hundredth. For one, on his bed, unable to walk, it had been 38 years. When Jesus stopped to ask him "Wilt thou be made whole?" (v. 6), he replied with the reason he was still waiting: he had no one to put him in that pool called Bethesda ("the house of mercy").

Another passerby might have chided the man for laziness. (*What's the matter with you? Why haven't you made it down to the water yet?*)

Another might have accused him of languishing there on purpose, for pity or for money. (*Quit feeling sorry for yourself! Get a job!*) Still another might have cited some sin. (*Surely this is the result of . . .*)

Jesus—mercy incarnate, asked only if the man wanted to be healed. The man yielded, took up his bed, and walked. Jesus asks the sick—and the sick at heart—the same question today.

Merciful Father, I yield to Your saving, healing, and transforming power today. In the holy name of Jesus, my Lord and Savior, I pray. Amen.

December 30, 31. **Phyllis Beveridge Nissila** is a writer and instructor at Lane Community College in Eugene, Oregon. She is married and the mother of two daughters.

Still Reverberating

It is a good thing to give thanks unto the Lord, and to sing praises unto thy name, O most High (Psalm 92:1, *King James Version*).

Scripture: Psalm 92:1-8
Song: "He Has Made Me Glad"

I grew up thinking religion was only about sitting up straight, minding the rules, and not asking questions. In church, I pictured God frowning on me with my smudged shoes, dirty fingernails, and sermon yawns.

My Sunday song was hardly the joyful Sabbath day psalm of David. It was more like a funeral dirge. The only thing I was happy about: soon the service would end. Then I could exchange my starchy Sunday clothes for jeans and a T-shirt and go back outdoors to play.

As I grew in the knowledge of God's Word, I came to realize it isn't about sitting up straight in a pew. No, it's about "[sitting] together in heavenly places in Christ Jesus" (Ephesians 2:6). It isn't about perfecting lists of rigid rules; rather, it's about the delight found in doing God's will and observing His law implanted in my heart (Psalm 40:6). It isn't about blind obedience, but about the freedom to ask, seek, and knock (Matthew 7:7, 8).

Because of the faithful tutelage of the Holy Spirit—not just one day a week, but every day—my sad song became a glad song. It reverberates still.

Thank You, **Lord,** for a new song in my heart—the song of new life, of forgiveness and adoption into Your family, of redemption and of the indwelling Spirit. Help me to sing joyfully of Your goodness, this day and every day! In Jesus' name, amen.

DEVOTIONS®

January

"Friend, your sins are forgiven."

—Luke 5:20

Gary Wilde, Editor   **Margaret Williams,** Project Editor   Photo John Foxx | Stockbyte | Thinkstock®

DEVOTIONS® is published quarterly by Standard Publishing, Cincinnati, Ohio, www.standardpub.com. © 2012 by Standard Publishing. All rights reserved. Topics based on the Home Daily Bible Readings, International Sunday School Lessons. © 2010 by the Committee on the Uniform Series. Printed in the U.S.A. All Scripture quotations, unless otherwise indicated, are taken from the *HOLY BIBLE, NEW INTERNATIONAL VERSION*®. *NIV*®. Copyright © 1973, 1978, 1984, 2011 by Biblica, Inc.™ Used by permission of Zondervan. All rights reserved. *King James Version* (*KJV*), public domain. The *New King James Version*. Copyright © 1982 by Thomas Nelson, Inc. *New American Standard Bible* (*NASB*), © The Lockman Foundation, 1960, 1962, 1963, 1968, 1971, 1972, 1973, 1975, 1977, 1995. Scripture quotations marked (*The Message*) are taken from *THE MESSAGE*. Copyright © by Eugene H. Peterson 1993, 1994, 1995, 1996, 2000, 2001, 2002. Used by permission of NavPress Publishing Group.

Resting in His Provision

So the people rested on the seventh day (Exodus 16:30).

Scripture: Exodus 16:22-30
Song: "Create in Me a Clean Heart"

Their marriage entered a mean season. He criticized. She snipped back. Her love for him withered . . . Then one day it occurred to her: God not only provided daily food for the Israelites in the desert, He preserved the perishable provision one extra day—the day they were not allowed to work. God's people got the rest they needed, and He provided the food they needed.

She wondered if God could help her love her husband again in the desert of her marriage. She wondered if somehow she could also obtain desperately needed mental and emotional rest in the meantime. "Lord," she prayed, "I no longer have a heart for my husband. Give me Your heart for him."

Day by week by month by year, she yielded more to the comfort and counsel of the Holy Spirit and less to the barbs of a critical spirit. Gradually, her peace returned. At length, from a position of rest, she was able to perceive her husband in a new light and to once again love him.

"As I committed to that prayer," she testified some years later, "I felt an immediate sense of relief. And even while our relationship was mending, I experienced the rest I so desperately needed." In time, her husband received a new heart for her too.

Lord, please give me Your heart for the one who is hurting me. If it's not Your will for me to leave, then give me all I need to stay, in peace. Through Christ, amen.

January 1–5. **Phyllis Beveridge Nissila** is a writer and instructor at Lane Community College in Eugene, Oregon. She is married and the mother of two daughters.

The Rest of the Story

The seventh day is the sabbath of the LORD thy God: in it thou shalt not do any work, thou, nor thy son, nor thy daughter, nor thy manservant, nor thy maidservant (Deuteronomy 5:14, *King James Version*).

Scripture: Deuteronomy 5:11-15
Song: "My Grandfather's Bible"

It's easy to think only of the "don't do that" part of God's commandments and rarely to consider the blessing part—the part where our obedience benefits not only our lives but the lives of others.

When we worship the true God, we don't fall into the deceptions of false gods, and we don't influence others to fall.

When we remain faithful in our marriage, we save our spouse and our children from anger and heartache, and we save another's loved ones from anger and heartache.

When we promote respect for what rightly belongs to people, we ensure that we, and others, retain the necessities of life.

When we tell the truth, we maintain our own dignity and honor, and we help preserve the dignity and honor of others.

When we choose life, we live, and so do others.

Today's verse gives us the fourth commandment, the Sabbath rest, and the benefits of observing that commandment are evident too. Not only is the immediate family of this household blessed, but so are all others in the house, including visitors.

Thank You, **Lord,** that the blessings of our obedience benefit not only us, but ripple outward to benefit our friends and relatives—and even those we may not know until eternity. Your goodness excels my comprehension! In Jesus' name, amen.

In Due Time

These are the feasts of the LORD, even holy convocations, which ye shall proclaim in their seasons (Leviticus 23:4, *King James Version*).

Scripture: Leviticus 23:1-8
Song: "In His Time"

One of God's gifts to mankind is timing. Timing helps us both anticipate and understand events. A baby takes nine months to gestate, for example, until its body parts and systems are complete. Timing also helps us believers comprehend God's plan for us, both historically and prophetically, as revealed in the feasts outlined in today's passage.

When Moses wrote Leviticus in the desert, the Israelites knew the historical import of the Feast of Passover. They understood it was a commemoration of their deliverance from the last plague visited upon Egypt. The blood of the sacrificial lamb, splashed on their doorposts, kept the angel of death away.

They also would have understood the historical significance of the Feast of Unleavened Bread. It commemorated that last week in slavery as well and the imminence of deliverance—no time for the yeast to rise!

Centuries later, we realize the prophetic import of those events too. Jesus is the spotless Passover lamb, who saves us from eternal destruction. Jesus is also the "unleavened bread," the yeast-free bread of life, who preserves us on our spiritual journey. In due time—God's time—all things come to pass.

Thank You, **Lord,** for Your perfect timing in fulfilling Your never-failing promises to Your people. In the precious name of Jesus, I offer my praise. Amen.

It All Starts Here

They obeyed not, neither inclined their ear, but made their neck stiff, that they might not hear, nor receive instruction (Jeremiah 17:23, *King James Version*).

Scripture: Jeremiah 17:19-27
Song: "I Choose Jesus"

When my daughters were young, they enjoyed a genre of books that invited them to choose their own, individualized adventures. When they got to page six, for example—the very point at which a hero could choose between the path to a castle on the right or the path to an enchanted forest on the left—the author invited them to turn to a page corresponding to their choice. The adventure shifted accordingly, and more exciting options awaited.

In today's passage, God offered a choice to His people too. The results of one of the choices, however, would be drastically different than in the children's books.

If the Israelites chose to obey Him, starting with the Sabbath rest, further instruction awaited them. Good results would ensue, as proclaimed by the prophet Jeremiah. If they chose, however, to ignore His command to honor the day of rest—and this, a command designed for their refreshment!—harm would befall them, the details of which were also foretold by Jeremiah.

We too have a choice today: life abundant in Christ Jesus or eternal separation from God's loving guidance and provision.

It all starts here.

Dear Father, help me choose Your will and Your way in all things today. Let me stop, amidst my busyness, to hear Your still, small voice. Through Christ, amen.

Sabbath Eyes

He said unto them, That the Son of man is Lord also of the sabbath (Luke 6:5, *King James Version*).

Scripture: Luke 6:1-11
Song: "Give Me, O Lord, a Heart of Grace"

Recently, I discovered "computer glasses." These yellow-tinted reading glasses are designed to ease eye strain at the word processor. Every time I don them, the effect on my hardworking eyes is dramatic. Instantly, my eyes feel refreshed.

The religious leaders in today's passage had, you might say, a strained view of the Sabbath commandment. They focused only on what "work" couldn't be done on that day of rest. Their list of forbidden activities even included necessities such as gathering food and healing the sick.

Along came Jesus, on the Sabbath, eating corn picked in a field and healing a man's withered hand. The Pharisees were enraged. Jesus reminded them, however, that King David had gathered food on the Sabbath. The Savior even performed a miracle in their midst. But the religious leaders, focused on their own interpretation of the commandment, remained blinded to its true meaning.

It's easy to don the lens of legalism and miss the true rest that comes by keeping our eyes on Jesus. It's easy to forget He finished, on the cross, the only work that matters, so that all who believe can enter into the true rest (Hebrews 4:3).

Almighty and most merciful Father, teach me how to rest in Your Son's finished work on the cross. In Him, I have the peace that passes understanding—and I am thankful! In the name of the Father, the Son, and the Holy Spirit, I pray. Amen.

Facing Injustice?

Let the LORD judge the peoples. Vindicate me, LORD, according to my righteousness, according to my integrity, O Most High (Psalm 7:8).

Scripture: Psalm 7:7-17
Song: "Defend Us, Lord, from Every Ill"

When our son was falsely accused of dishonesty on his job, I became angry and wanted to tell his accusers a thing or two. One day in the grocery store, my anger reached a peak. *If I get a wobbly cart, I'll be mad,* I thought, jerking a cart from the racks.

As I pushed my cart down an aisle, two people blocked my way. *Can't they see I'm in a hurry?* One women moved and smiled an apology. I didn't smile back. As I reached into the dairy case, I sensed a voice saying, "Let it go. Let the anger and hurt go. That's not my way."

David, too, faced the pain of injustice when he was accused of trying to kill King Saul and seize the throne. It wasn't true, and he cried out to God. From his prayer, we gain insight into how we can react when falsely accused. Don't waste time brooding over false accusations or devising ways to get even. Instead, ask God to plead your case and restore your reputation. In His own time, in His own way, a just God promises to deal with unjust people and situations. (And remember the role of your own compassion: It's wounded people who wound others.)

Lord God, You are my defender. You will vindicate me and my loved ones in Your own good time. Thank You, through Christ my Lord. Amen.

January 6–12. **Jewell Johnson** lives in Arizona with her husband, LeRoy. They are parents to six children and grandparents to nine. Besides writing, Jewell enjoys walking, reading, and quilting.

God's Rescue Plan

The righteous person is rescued from trouble, and it falls on the wicked instead (Proverbs 11:8).

Scripture: Proverbs 11:3-11
Song: "A Mighty Fortress Is Our God"

When Jonathan Goforth went as a missionary to China in 1888, he had a difficult time learning the language. This was not a problem for fellow-missionary, Donald McGullivray, however, who arrived in China a year later than Goforth. "We don't understand you. Let McGullivray preach," the people told Goforth when he attempted to preach.

Goforth felt like a failure. Then one day something happened. He told his wife, "I began to speak, and the phrases and idioms that always eluded me came easily." He recorded the incident in his diary. Two months later a letter came from students attending a Canadian Bible college. At a prayer meeting, the students had been impressed to pray especially for Goforth.

The weapon of prayer—thrust at discouragement—had provided the breakthrough. When Goforth checked his diary, he saw that the day the students prayed corresponded with the time he began experiencing freedom with the Chinese language.

Difficulties confront believers and unbelievers alike, but Christians have spiritual weapons with which to overcome their problems. This week read Ephesians 6:10-18 and use God's defense plan often to rescue others—and yourself—from impossible circumstances.

Lord, I'm no match for the discouragements and inadequacies that often plague me. But with Your armor in place, I will confront them boldly today. Through Christ, amen.

Apply This Truth!

You have been set free from sin and have become slaves to righteousness (Romans 6:18).

Scripture: Romans 6:16-23
Song: "Shining for Jesus"

Margo is a beautician. She makes a living cutting and styling people's hair and giving manicures. But she does more than that.

When she felt led by the Lord to begin a women's prayer meeting in her church, she obeyed. Now every week she leads several ladies as they pray for world and local needs.

Then a desire grew in Margo's heart to learn sign language. Although there are presently no deaf people in her church, each week she practices the signs for the songs and accompanies the worship team. Margo could easily allow work, entertainment, and family to absorb her time and energy, but as a Christian, she walks in obedience to another voice.

Christians are no longer slaves to a wholly self-absorbed life. God has saved us to accomplish His purpose: To reach the world with the good news of Jesus. How He accomplishes the work through us will vary with each person. He may impress on us, His servants, a desire to learn a new skill, go on a mission trip, teach the church nursery children, or become involved in other outreach efforts.

"Saved to serve" isn't just a cliché. It's a down-to-earth biblical truth, ready for our personal, unique applications.

Speak, **Lord,** for Your servant is listening. Today I want to hear Your wisdom and guidance. How shall I use my gifts today? Where is the need? Who will be blessed? I pray this prayer in the name of Jesus, my Savior and Lord. Amen.

Make Beautiful Music

Live such good lives among the pagans that, though they accuse you of doing wrong, they may see your good deeds and glorify God on the day he visits us (1 Peter 2:12).

Scripture: 1 Peter 2:11-17
Song: "Take My Life and Let It Be"

Antonio Stradivari, Italian maker of stringed instruments in the eighteenth century, worked to perfect the violin and cello. The woods he used—maple, spruce, and willow—were carefully chosen and treated. He refused to sell an instrument until it was near perfect. "If my violins are defective, God's music will be spoiled," he said. He made over a thousand instruments in his lifetime. About 650 survive today and sell for a small fortune.

The apostle Peter wrote to believers scattered by persecution. Now they were enduring opposition from the Roman government under Nero. Yet Peter encouraged them to live their lives with the pagan population in mind. Even if these Christians were accused of wrongdoing, their good lives would speak loudly to onlookers.

As witnesses for Christ, we do not want "God's music" to be spoiled by a shoddy lifestyle. Yet, while we may avoid blatant sins, we might engage in more "acceptable" sins such as speaking critically of others or telling "little white lies." Not everyone reads the Bible, so our lives may be the only "Word" our neighbors and coworkers ever know. Let us play beautiful melodies to the watching world.

Almighty God, I long for my life to bear witness to Your goodness and grace. Reveal to me areas that may hinder my testimony. In Jesus' name, amen.

Forgive Quickly

"Lord, how many times shall I forgive my brother or sister who sins against me? Up to seven times?" Jesus answered, "I tell you, not seven times, but seventy-seven times" (Matthew 18:21, 22).

Scripture: Matthew 18:21-35
Song: "I Want to Be Like Jesus"

When our daughter Jenny auditioned for all-state chorus, I knew she'd be chosen. Why not? She read music easily and had a pleasant alto voice.

To my amazement, she was *not* the teacher's choice. Jenny accepted the decision, but I just couldn't. Day after day I entertained angry thoughts. In fact, I could hardly read my Bible for thinking of the injustice. "Just wait until the next parent-teacher conference," I told my husband. "I'll really give that teacher a piece of my mind."

Soon bitterness held me in its grip. Have you noticed that an unforgiving attitude has a way of taking over? No wonder Jesus told Peter to place no limits on the times we forgive.

Equally important is to forgive quickly after an offense. Harboring an unforgiving spirit produces a domino effect. We choose not to forgive, then we become bitter. Hatred is the next step on the downward spiral. Soon we may entertain violent thoughts toward the one who offended us.

So how do we forgive those who hurt us? We give our anger to God—once, twice, a hundred times a day, if necessary.

Lord, You willingly forgive my sins when I confess them. Now I offer the same forgiveness to those who have offended me. In the name of Jesus, amen.

Specks and Planks

First take the plank out of your eye, and then you will see clearly to remove the speck from your brother's eye (Luke 6:42).

Scripture: Luke 6:37-42
Song: "Search Me, O God"

Carla, a children's Sunday school teacher, was late for class almost every Sunday. Her students would sit in my classroom waiting for her to appear—which was usually 15 minutes after the bell rang. I became critical of Carla, not to her face, but in my spirit. *Why is she always tardy? Why does the superintendent allow her to teach when she can't be on time?*

Then I heard Carla had a chronic illness that caused her great discomfort. Although I never heard her complain, I learned that it was quite difficult for her to get moving in the morning. Perhaps she shouldn't be teaching, but I had no business finding fault with her.

My point: There are *reasons* for people's flaws and failures. And, because we do not know what another person is dealing with, let us not judge them by our imperfect standards. Often when we call attention to the faults of others, we are covering up similar shortcomings in ourselves.

When we set ourselves up as a judge, we take on the role of God. Our only obligation to those who seem "less than perfect" is to love them sincerely, just as we love our less-than-perfect selves.

Merciful God, forgive me for the habit of judging people. With Your help, I will enfold them with love as You enfold me, imperfect as I am. Through Christ I pray, amen.

Dealing with Our Enemies

Love your enemies, do good to those who hate you, bless those who curse you, pray for those who mistreat you (Luke 6:27, 28).

Scripture: Luke 6:12, 13, 17-31
Song: "Blest Are the Pure in Heart"

During the 1940s, Jewish people were targeted for extermination by the Nazis. Corrie ten Boom and her family hid Jews in their home in Holland during this era and because of their efforts, lives were spared. When their work became known to the Nazis, the ten Booms were imprisoned. Her father and sister died in concentration camps while Corrie survived and went on to preach in 60 countries.

After Corrie had preached at a meeting in Munich, a man extended his hand to her. Corrie recognized him as a former SS guard at Ravensbruck, the prison where her sister had died. Angry thoughts flooded Corrie's mind. Yet when she grasped his hand, a current seemed to pass between them. She couldn't forgive him, but Jesus in her could.

Our human reaction to "enemies" is to hold grudges and attempt to get even. In contrast, Jesus gave us a fourfold plan for dealing with those we'd prefer to curse: He said love these people, do good to them, bless them, and pray for them.

Each act mirrors the actions of our master. It is easy to wound others when we have been wounded. It takes Christ within us to respond as He did.

Heavenly Father, I do not feel love for persons who hurt me, but with Your help, I will show them Your love. In my merciful Savior's name I pray. Amen.

Save Me from Pride

How art thou fallen from heaven, O Lucifer, son of the morning! How art thou cut down to the ground, which didst weaken the nations! For thou hast said in thine heart, I will ascend into heaven (Isaiah 14:12, *King James Version*).

Scripture: Isaiah 14:12-20
Song: "Depth of Mercy"

For a number of years, I was a journalist in a small town with a big university. As the reporter who covered the university, I had access to many "important" people. When I would call the president of the university, he'd take my call. If I had a question, people would work to find answers. At the time, I didn't think all this was going to my head.

Then I left the newspaper. And, I discovered, I no longer mattered! When I ran into a high-ranking official of the school at a grocery store, he acted as if he'd never met me. A few months earlier, he would have treated me like an old friend. That stung.

The hurt I felt was my wounded pride, and this first of the deadly sins can easily infect our lives. Too often we find ourselves thinking too highly of ourselves, forgetting that every thing we have and are is a gift from God. When God knocks us back down to earth—as He did the prideful Lucifer—we should be grateful for the opportunity to live with a little more thankfulness. (Sadly, that didn't work with the son of the morning.)

Father, open my eyes to the ways I let pride get in the way of my love of You. Restore in me a grateful heart and a humble spirit. Through Christ I pray. Amen.

January 13–19. **John Meunier** is a part-time minister and a lecturer in Business Communication at Indiana University in Bloomington.

God on the Line

Humble yourselves before the Lord, and he will lift you up (James 4:10).

Scripture: James 4:7-12
Song: "Be Still, My Soul"

Andy was not a patient fisherman. He was only 10, so that was understandable. His impatience led to a theory. He decided that if he threw a rock into the lake—the bigger the better—the fish would get curious about what made the splash. They would come to investigate. So, Andy would throw a rock and then cast his line into the spot where the rock had hit the water.

Not a lot of people wanted to fish with Andy.

But how many of us treat our life with God the same way? We grow impatient. We chafe at the idea that God might deem it best to make us wait. We pick up rocks and throw them in the lake on the theory that our outbursts will get God's attention.

James teaches us what experienced anglers know. If you want to catch a fish, you must be humble enough to understand how a fish lives. You have to submit, let your actions and expectations grow out of the life of fish. (And fish certainly don't want rocks raining down on them!)

It is the same with God. When we humble ourselves to wait on God, to be patient for God, and to be attentive to God, that is when He shows up in His own time.

My soul can be so restless at times, **Father.** I want You to respond on my time. I want You to work on my schedule. Help me, Lord, to find the humility to wait on You. Let me stand before the still waters and wait for You. In the name of Jesus, who lives and reigns with You and the Holy Spirit, now and forever, amen.

Cast Your Cares upon Him

Cast all your anxiety on him because he cares for you (1 Peter 5:7).

Scripture: 1 Peter 5:1-7
Song: "Cares Chorus"

Anna prayed every day. She offered God her praise; she handed over her worries and cares—or most of them, anyway. When it came to her son, there were some things she just could not hand over. His alcoholism, his failed marriage, and his wandering away from the faith of his childhood—these were all too big to give over to God. She never said it this way, but a wise friend named it right: She thought these worries were too big for God. She would bear them instead.

You know what happened. The burden of those worries, her deep fears and anxieties, ground Anna down. It turned out that she was wrong. They were not too big for God. They were too big for her.

Can you relate? I know I can be like Anna. I hold back when God asks me for all of my anxieties and cares. I give him some, but I hold on to some, as well. Some of our fears just seem too big or too important or too close to our hearts to hand over to God.

Yet, I know: No pain, no fear, no worry, no anxiety of ours is too big for God. Nothing that we place on God's shoulders is worse than what He willingly took upon himself for our sake. Cast your cares upon Him.

Father, I know You ask me to give all my cares to You. I know, but my heart wants to hold on. Give me the courage and faith to let go today! In Jesus' name, amen.

More Than Just the News

The LORD builds up Jerusalem; he gathers the exiles of Israel (Psalm 147:2).

Scripture: Psalm 147:1-11
Song: "Battle Hymn of the Republic"

As Abraham Lincoln rose to give his second inaugural address in 1865, the end of the Civil War was in sight, but not yet reached. Bloody battle had cost the lives of thousands upon thousands. And it would demand many more. The president knew this as he spoke to a nation weary of war.

"Fondly do we hope—fervently do we pray—that this mighty scourge of war may speedily pass away. Yet, if God wills that it continue, until all the wealth piled by the bond-man's two hundred and fifty years of unrequited toil shall be sunk, and until every drop of blood drawn with the lash, shall be paid by another drawn with the sword, as was said three thousand years ago, so still it must be said 'the judgments of the Lord are true and righteous altogether.'"

God is not just a God for the quiet morning of our prayers and our worship on Sunday morning. He is the God of all. He is the God of our nation and world. When hardship comes to a nation, God is working. When prosperity comes, God is working. As God's people, we see Him at work where others see merely the news of the day. As it was in the days of ancient Israel, so it is today: The Lord builds up and gathers, in His sovereign wisdom.

God of wisdom and might, You rule the nations with truth and love. Help me to see in the news of this day Your hand at work, leading, judging, and loving Your world— or simply showing great and gracious restraint . . . for now. Through Christ, amen.

Enjoy Your Creator!

From the rising of the sun to the place where it sets, the name of the LORD is to be praised (Psalm 113:3).

Scripture: Psalm 113
Song: "For the Beauty of the Earth"

Joan loved the dirt. She loved to plant seeds in the ground and watch them grow. As a master gardener, she thrived on weeding and pruning. So, naturally, she took care of the plants on the church grounds and kept an eagle eye on the man the congregation had hired to mow the grass.

But Joan could be a bit of a tyrant when it came to the annual spring workday. She wouldn't tolerate a sloppy job as she watched volunteers spreading mulch or trimming spruce hedges. No one was immune to her wagging finger and knit brow when she thought the work wasn't up to par.

One fine spring day, an exasperated church member threw his trowel to the ground after one of Joan's mini-lectures. "Why do you make such a big deal about it?" he asked.

"George," she said. "God made that bush beautiful for us to look at and for all kinds of creatures to nest in. The least we can do is see that its feet stay warm."

Joan understood that every corner of God's creation is a testimony to His love. We who live in this beautiful earth are reminded to receive each and every piece of it as a gift. We praise the Lord when we care for it. (And Joan: relax, *enjoy!*)

Creator God, before there were nations and before You made us, You made this glorious world. Help me, Lord, to praise You for each gift, from the rising of the sun to its setting each day of my life. In Jesus' name, amen.

A Clean Heart

Because of your stubbornness and your unrepentant heart, you are storing up wrath against yourself for the day of God's wrath, when his righteous judgment will be revealed (Romans 2:5).

Scripture: Romans 2:1-11
Song: "And Can It Be?"

Doug didn't like his heart surgeon. The man was always giving him a hard time. Stop smoking. Stop eating cheeseburgers. Stop with the deep-fried foods. "If you keep on like this," he told Doug, "there won't be anything I can do for you."

"I'd rather live a happy life than a long one," Doug used to say. Sadly, he got his wish. Ten days short of his 61st birthday, the massive heart attack his doctor had been warning him about struck in the middle of his morning shower.

Too often we live as if our actions and our choices have no consequences. And we lash out with anger at anyone who points out the truth to us. Whether it is a doctor, a fellow Christian, or the apostle Paul, we turn a deaf ear. But the day of reckoning will arrive.

The good news is that we have a heart surgeon of another kind. Jesus Christ can clean the blockages in the vessels of our spirit and give us a renewed heart, if we will turn to Him. When the preacher reminds us of sin, it is the voice of Doug's heart surgeon calling him to lay down the smokes. He is warning us of the day to come and offering us a cure that never fails.

Father, You know my transgressions. You can purify my heart. By the blood of Your Son, my Savior, make me clean today. Through Christ I pray. Amen.

At the Table, Together

When you give a banquet, invite the poor, the crippled, the lame, the blind (Luke 14:13).

Scripture: Luke 14:7-18, 21-24
Song: "Come, Sinners, to the Gospel Feast"

Peter Storey was a bishop in South Africa during the height of apartheid. One night, visiting in a prison, he spoke with a black minister who had been arrested. As Storey prepared to offer the man communion, he turned to the white prison guard and invited him to join as well.

Storey said that it is a tradition that the least among us be served first, and so he offered the bread and cup to the black prisoner. He then offered them to the white guard.

The guard found himself suddenly torn. To drink after a black man would be an outrage to him. To refuse the cup of Christ would be an affront to God. After a moment of indecision, he drank. For a few moments, at least, the two men were brothers at the Lord's table.

Who we share a table with says a lot about us. Jesus taught His disciples always to include the poor, the disabled, and the suffering at the banquets of life.

It makes me wonder: Where in my life are the people whom God is inviting to fellowship with Him—and with me? If I will open my eyes to see them, I'll find many in need of food, of clean water, and of a genuine friendship. As God's people, I know I'm called to seek them out and bring them to the table with me.

Lord, open my eyes to see the hungry in the world around me. Open my heart so I might feed them out of the bounty You have given me. Through Christ, amen.

Open Your Hand

You shall open your hand wide to [the poor one] and willingly lend him sufficient for his need, whatever he needs (Deuteronomy 15:8, *New King James Version*).

Scripture: Deuteronomy 15:7-11
Song: "People Need the Lord"

The tiny hut sat in the center of an east African village. As the national host led us through the circle of thatched huts, an elderly woman burst through an open doorway and ran up the path toward us.

"Jambo," she cried in greeting, grasping our hands. The host told us that missionaries had never visited this village before. The woman was beside herself with joy at our presence.

It was a humbling experience, especially when the village people all began to bring gifts and lay them before us. Gifts given out of their poverty. And they each insisted that we lay a hand upon the head of each village child "to bless them."

It was my first of many trips to Kenya, each a soul-shaking experience that never failed to stir me. And today I am again reminded to open my heart and hands, not only in lands abroad, but on my own turf as well.

People need the Lord, and we need not fear giving too much. But like the Israelites in our Scripture, we must beware giving too little.

Father, please make me a vehicle of blessing to others; and may I be sensitive to respond to the needs around me. In Jesus' name, amen.

January 20–26. **Penny Smith,** freelance writer and speaker, has two married sons and lives in Harrisburg, Pennsylvania, with her two Bichon pups.

Caught in the Act

He need not further consider a man, that he should go before God in judgment (Job 34:23, *New King James Version*).

Scripture: Job 34:17-30
Song: "Freedom"

I never liked jury duty, but here I was again. The first case was easy: a shoplifter caught in the act. The second case, however, had been more challenging for the jurors. When a chunk of someone's future is in your hands, you feel as if you're swallowing an apple whole. (Gulp.)

We next carefully considered a drug case, and it brought back painful memories. I found it difficult to concentrate on the pro-and-con arguments in the jury room. My thoughts kept tugging me back to a prison cell where a close relative had served time for drug possession.

Job's comforters claimed that the Almighty hears the cry of the afflicted. From Job's perspective it didn't seem true. Yet Job had cried, "Though he slay me, yet will I hope in him" (Job 13:15). When problems escalate, will we yet believe in the goodness of God?

The drug addict was convicted of the charges against him. But the judge sent him to a drug rehabilitation program rather than to prison. He received another chance for a future.

In a sense, we have all been caught in the act. Yet we believers receive another chance because of Christ—because of the verdict that comes to us by His work on the cross: "Not guilty!"

Thank You, **Father,** for the liberating redemption won for me by the blood of Your Son! I can only respond with a life of humble gratitude. In Jesus' name, amen.

A Little Bit of Greed?

He said this, not because he was concerned about the poor, but because he was a thief, and as he had the money box, he used to pilfer what was put into it (John 12:6, *New American Standard Bible*).

Scripture: John 12:1-8
Song: "Loyalty to Christ"

The Gospel account is clear: Jesus knew the moment Judas betrayed him (see John 13:18-27). The dishonesty of Judas was like a disease that ate away at his character, as he walked the path of unrepentant sin . . . toward judgment.

Judgment is a fearsome thing, but salvation is a matter of choice, offered to all. That is the wonderful hope to which every Christian holds tightly. It is the same hope that Mary demonstrated when she poured out extravagant devotion at the feet of Jesus. Unknowingly, she prepared the Lord for the burial of His body on earth.

Likewise, our extravagant devotion to the Lord will keep us pure in heart. But let us always be aware that "sin crouching at the door" (Genesis 4:7) of our lives. It may start with just a little bit of greed—no doubt the way it crept into Judas's soul. His secret life led him to the brutality of robbery, even from the very poor. Whenever and wherever deception and dishonesty enter—whether in society or in the church—there the character of Judas is emerging.

My dear heavenly Father, help me to walk in Your ways with a true heart. Fill me with Your Spirit that I may reflect Your character for Your glory. In the name of the Father and of the Son and of the Holy Spirit, I pray. Amen.

Arrest His Attention!

Zacchaeus, make haste and come down, for today I must stay at your house (Luke 19:5, *New King James Version*).

Scripture: Luke 19:1-10
Song: "Visit Us"

The room was packed full, and with great detail I described the scene. I said, "Brother Zack was so short that the only way he could hope to see Jesus above the heads of the crowd was to climb a tree." As I was speaking, a gentleman entered the room, and seeing all the seats were taken, he ascended the open stairwell and sat on the top step. The irony of the situation is that the man was less than five feet tall. Show and tell!

Red-faced and stuttering—but realizing it was too late to back out—I continued: "Visitation is based on our desire to see Him," and the brother on the stairs beamed.

A "visitation of the Lord" is one way we might describe the spiritual release that comes when we determine to do whatever it takes to experience Him. Jesus chose to visit the home of Zacchaeus because of the man's obvious desire for such fellowship.

Even today, with us, the Lord comes close—and with a plan to stay, to abide (see John 15). But He also promises special "times of refreshing" from His presence (see Acts 3:10) that can break into our day at any time. That kind of "visitation" happens when we spend time in His Word and in prayer. We will arrest His attention when we give Him ours.

O gracious God, I turn from my insufficiency and crowded circumstances today, to see You at work in my life. Help me to be conscious of Your presence each hour of this day. In the name of Jesus, Lord and Savior of all, I pray. Amen.

Do We Get It?

The master commended the unjust steward because he had dealt shrewdly. For the sons of this world are more shrewd in their generation than the sons of light (Luke 16:8, *New King James Version*).

Scripture: Luke 16:1-9
Song: "Give Me Thy Heart"

The United States is probably the world's greatest offender when it comes to waste. We seem to have little concern for starving populations while we fill our dumpsters with edible food and usable materials.

The group of teens that accompanied me on a missionary trip to the hills of Haiti received a new perspective on stewardship and waste. They learned that not everyone has a soft bed — or even one meal a day. Drinking water had to be boiled, and there was very little of it for bathing. Travel accommodations inland were difficult, at best. Poverty surrounded us.

Our visit to an orphanage capped it. Small children slept on concrete floors and maybe ate one meal daily. In the overcrowded house, the children, faces smeared from running noses, raised their hands to be lifted. The teens obliged with tears streaking their own cheeks as they cuddled the children. Now they got it.

The team arrived home with a mission on their hearts. They now took seriously what Jesus had to say about giving and became faithful stewards of their allowances and earnings from part-time jobs. Bottom line: Stewardship replaced selfishness.

Lord, You have blessed me beyond measure. I want to be a wise steward, regardless of my circumstances. Immerse me in Your mercy, for Jesus' sake. Amen.

He Sees Inside

He said to them, "You are those who justify yourselves before men, but God knows your hearts. For what is highly esteemed among men is an abomination in the sight of God" (Luke 16:15, *New King James Version*).

Scripture: Luke 16:10-18
Song: "Purify My Heart"

After my message one of the missionaries approached me with a chuckle. "That's a nice broach you're wearing." Now I knew that I wore no jewelry because it happened to be taboo here. An evidence of regeneration among this particular tribe was the surrender of ornamental jewelry, and the missionaries honored the tribal custom (see 1 Corinthians 8:13).

The missionary pointed to my jacket lapel—and there sat a monstrous, colorful roach! He informed me that it had rested there throughout the entire message. Fortunately, I was completely unaware, or I would have added sound effects to the message.

Sometimes our view of ourselves is a far cry from what others see. We may either underestimate or overestimate ourselves. The Pharisees were in the latter group. Jesus "bumped their cup," but they would not acknowledge their greed and dishonesty. *The Message* translation of the Bible calls the Pharisees "a money-obsessed bunch." Jesus knew what was inside their hearts. And, as it is with us, when that "inner cup" is bumped, what's inside spills out for all to see.

Lord, I bless Your name for Your faithfulness. Help me to live with integrity of heart that I may be faithful in all my ways, by Your grace. Through Christ, amen.

Why Not Err on the Side of Mercy?

I beg you therefore, father, that you would send him to my father's house (Luke 16:27, *New King James Version*).

Scripture: Luke 16:19-31
Song: "Mercy Is Boundless and Free"

Our church is the first one listed in the yellow pages, and we receive many calls for financial help. We're only too anxious to assist with any legitimate need, yet people are disappointed when we give food or a gift card. You see, we're aware that cash will often be spent on tobacco, alcohol, or drugs.

One mother of three preschoolers was desperate. No food, no fuel, and definitely no fun. She had applied for government assistance, but the process was slow. She didn't know where to turn . . . when she finally looked in the yellow pages.

To ignore such need would be cold and heartless—acting as the rich man did in our Scripture today. So we helped the best we could.

This young mother then offered to pay back what we had contributed. Her heart was right. She also realized that she needed to identify with a local church and include God in her life. Soon she would have a whole family of supportive brothers and sisters in Christ.

The account in Luke may have turned out differently had the rich man extended mercy to Lazarus. No doubt they would have been enjoying the glories of Heaven together. If we are going to err, it is better to err on the side of mercy.

Blessed Lord, in these times of economic stress, help us not to withhold from others the mercy that You wish to extend through us. In the holy name of Jesus, amen.

Shame on You!

This is what the LORD Almighty, the God of Israel, says: Go ahead, add your burnt offerings to your other sacrifices and eat the meat yourselves! (Jeremiah 7:21).

Scripture: Jeremiah 7:21-28
Song: "Each Step I Take"

Did you notice the exclamation mark at the end of verse 21? To me, it's as if the Lord's telling the Israelites: Go ahead, do whatever you want. (But be ready for the consequences.)

Oh, the strong hand of discipline when we make unwise decisions. "I have been watching! declares the Lord," (Jeremiah 7:11). In my generation, it was all about the look. My dad was a man of few words, and the look usually sufficed when we kids needed a little settling down.

Mom, on the other hand, was sometimes a pushover. I truly believe she gleaned her favorite disciplinary words straight from the Bible. For instance, Mom: "How many times do I have to tell you?" God: "I spoke to you again and again, but you did not listen" (Jeremiah 7:13). Mom: "Behave yourself and you can go play." God: "Reform your ways and your actions, and I will let you live in this place" (Jeremiah 7:3). Mom: "Do what you want. You're only hurting yourself." God: "Are they not rather harming themselves, to their own shame?" (Jeremiah 7:19).

Abba, Father, I praise Your holy name. I know Your discipline is for my own good. Help me to reform and change my ways. Teach me to listen. I give thanks for the peace and blessing I will receive when I obey. In Jesus' name, amen.

January 27–January 31. **Shirley J. Conley** is a freelance writer living in Central Florida. She enjoys writing devotionals and creative nonfiction. Her hobbies are gardening and sewing.

His Love

As for God, his way is perfect: The LORD's word is flawless; he shields all who take refuge in him (2 Samuel 22:31).

Scripture: 2 Samuel 22:26-31
Song: "Love Lifted Me"

I slid into my best shoes and grabbed my purse, Bible, and notebook. Then, rushing from the room, I stumbled . . . and stumbled again. I struggled to regain my balance, gripped my load tighter, and fought to retrieve my footing. *Who will pick me up?*

I live alone, and on occasion I've longed for someone to pick me up when my clumsiness got the better of me. Oh, how I wish I could see—as if on film—the fancy footwork that kept me from colliding with the hardwood floor that day! I think it would give me a good chuckle now.

As a Christian, I've often fallen short of what I believe God expects of me. When I think about that, a wave of self-pity can fill me. *Self-pity*—what an ugly word. And without a doubt it falls into the "flawed human being" category. I'm sure the Lord doesn't admire this trait in me.

On that day of my un-ballerina-like stumble, I rubbed my sprained foot and asked the Lord: "But who will pick me up next time?" I cried aloud as tears blurred my vision.

"I will," God gently whispered. And once more, I know I can rest assured in His promise: He will never leave me. (He even kept me from landing on the floor.)

O God, thank You for reminding me that You remain my shield. Your love lifts me up from my own faults when they threaten to drag me into the pit of self-pity. Thank You for never getting tired of picking me up when I stumble. Through Christ, amen.

Tell Them

Go near and listen to all that the LORD our God says. Then tell us whatever the LORD our God tells you. We will listen and obey (Deuteronomy 5:27).

Scripture: Deuteronomy 5:22-27
Song: "I Love to Tell the Story"

Evan dropped his grandmother's hand and came to stand in front of the lady on the workout machine beside me. His large brown eyes sparkled, and his grin magnified the dimples in his cherubic face. He looked into her eyes. With childlike confidence, he said, "When you die, you're going to Heaven." The lady to whom his prophecy was directed answered with a simple, "Thank you." Without another word, 3-year-old Evan returned to his grandmother's hand as he left the fitness center.

What prompted the child to speak those words to his chosen woman? Is he a modern-day prophet? Is it something he learned in church, and it continued to dwell on his mind? And what made him choose this *particular* lady? (This started me wondering whether Jesus was like Evan at the age of 3.)

In Mark 10:15, Jesus said, "Truly I tell you, anyone who will not receive the kingdom of God like a little child will never enter it." Scripture tells us to listen to the Lord and spread the good news to all the people. We adults should exhibit the courage to approach strangers with words of hope in our struggling world.

O God, the king of glory, teach me to listen and obey. Give me the boldness to go into a sometimes hostile world with Your words of hope and love. Help me to leave fear behind and go forward in faith, so others will know the wonders of Your love. I pray this prayer in the name of Jesus, my merciful Savior and Lord. Amen.

Teach the Children

Do not forget the things your eyes have seen or let them fade from your heart as long as you live. Teach them to your children and to their children after them (Deuteronomy 4:9).

Scripture: Deuteronomy 4:1-10
Song: "Everything Is Beautiful"

"My baby just pee-peed on the potty!" Pride and excitement resonated through the text message sent by my granddaughter, Savannah. I laughed when I saw the accompanying photo of 19-month-old Alexis; her grin reflected her mama's glee.

This started me thinking about what we teach our children — the basics: to walk and talk, to feed and dress themselves, and of course, the potty training. But how much do we teach them about God? (How pleased I was when my granddaughter, Shelby, at the age of 12, recited the books of the Bible.)

As a young child I said the prayer, "Now I lay me down to sleep." I later learned John 3:16, the Lord's Prayer, the 23rd Psalm, and the Ten Commandments. But I still can't recite the books of the Bible.

Now I'm a great-grandmother, and I've returned to Scripture to find out what I should teach the children. On my smartphone, I searched for "teach the children" and came up with 15 Scriptures. All but one was about teaching our children to love and obey God and His laws. However, my personal favorite is Proverbs 22:6, "Start children off on the way they should go, and even when they are old they will not turn from it."

Father, let Your Spirit overflow in me. I want to be a light shining for You in the lives of the little children You've placed in my life. I pray in Jesus' name. Amen.

Hungry for More

They claim to know God, but by their actions they deny him (Titus 1:16).

Scripture: Titus 1:10-16
Song: "Anywhere with Jesus"

"Good morning, Sweetpea," a middle-aged, stout and balding gentleman greeted me at the entrance to the church. *Sweetpea?* I've been called many things, but this was a first. Not sure how to respond, I smiled and accepted his hand. Would this greeting fit with the essential qualities Charles Swindoll included in his article, "How to Recognize a Healthy Church?" I wondered about it as I entered this place of worship for the first time.

My deep desire to let the Holy Spirit have more influence in my life had led me to visit a number of churches. I wanted to expand my biblical knowledge while serving the community. Even more, I needed a church where my soul would be fed as I worshipped in awe of God.

I found that most churches have kept up with technology, making some of them seem impersonal. For example, in this church I never actually met the minister, though I received a welcoming "form letter" by e-mail later in the week. Consequently, I browsed the church's website to discover its core values. As a result, I attended this church for many months—and although some of my needs were met, I never quite felt as if I belonged. I've never been part of planting a church, but my journey has helped me understand the struggles Titus faced.

Lord, I ask for Your guidance and wisdom as You lead me on this journey. May I never lose the love of the Holy Spirit planted in my heart. In Jesus' name, amen.

DEVOTIONS®

February

> This is how we know what love is: Jesus Christ laid down his life for us.
>
> —*1 John 3:16*

Gary Wilde, Editor   **Margaret Williams,** Project Editor   Photo iStockphoto | Thinkstock®

DEVOTIONS® is published quarterly by Standard Publishing, Cincinnati, Ohio, www.standardpub.com.
© 2012 by Standard Publishing. All rights reserved. Topics based on the Home Daily Bible Readings,
International Sunday School Lessons. © 2010 by the Committee on the Uniform Series. Printed in
the U.S.A. All Scripture quotations, unless otherwise indicated, are taken from the *HOLY BIBLE,
NEW INTERNATIONAL VERSION*®. *NIV*®. Copyright © 1973, 1978, 1984, 2011 by Biblica, Inc.™
Used by permission of Zondervan. All rights reserved. *The New King James Version*. Copyright ©
1982 by Thomas Nelson, Inc.

Heart Love

This is how we know what love is: Jesus Christ laid down his life for us (1 John 3:16).

Scripture: 1 John 3:14-20
Song: "Lord of Our Life and God of Our Salvation"

It's been said that music is a window to the soul. "How He Loves," written by songwriter John Mark McMillan, certainly touches my soul. It's been my message from God—like a trail of bread crumbs leading me to where He wants me.

My hunger—to let the indwelling Holy Spirit have more of me—persuaded me to search for another church. I never dreamed it would be so difficult. I'd entered this quest the first time I heard "How He Loves," and I thought *Surely this is the church for me.* It wasn't.

After many prayers, I attended another church and joined a women's Bible study that included a Christ-centered exercise and stretching class. During a period of meditation, music softly played in the background . . . God spoke to me through the words of the song.

Not knowing the name of the song, fragments of lyrics spun through my mind until I could no longer stand it. Needing to know the words, I searched iTunes until . . . yes! . . . I found it. Over and over I listened—and worshipped from the heart.

Father God, sometimes I forget, during the hurricanes of life, how much You love me. You gave Your life for me, and I give my life to You. In Jesus' name, amen.

February 1, 2. **Shirley J. Conley** is a freelance writer living in Central Florida. She enjoys writing devotionals and creative nonfiction. Her hobbies are gardening and sewing.

The Implanted Word

Do not merely listen to the word, and so deceive yourselves. Do what it says (James 1:22).

Scripture: James 1:19-27
Song: "Who Keepeth Not God's Word"

The Bible: a precious treasure to some, unimportant to others. A minister once asked several people what one hand-carried item they would take with them if they were exiled to a deserted island. The answers varied from a Boy-Scout knife to matches. Without hesitation, one woman answered, "My Bible. It would entertain me, teach me, bring comfort through the lonely days and nights, and remind me that I'm not alone."

I thought about this some years later when I truly took notice of a homeless man. Each day as I left the parking garage on my way to work, I saw him huddled in a doorway, an island unto himself. His wrinkled shirt hung sloppily below a dirty green jacket. A sweat-stained baseball cap kept his long, dirty hair from his eyes, while a straggly beard covered his face. The shopping bag beside him held his worldly possessions.

What drew my attention to this man? What made him stand out from the many homeless people wandering the streets by day and sleeping in doorways of the city at night? It was the Bible he hovered over. I could tell it wasn't just a Bible like we often give to those in need, but a well-worn personal book. He held the Bible in his lap and humbly received the Word of God.

Gracious Heavenly Father, let me receive Your Word in the same manner as those who cling to the Bible as their only and most treasured possession. I pray that the Holy Spirit will implant the Word in my heart. In the name of Jesus. Amen.

Anybody Here Indispensable?

How can I alone bear your problems and burdens and your complaints? (Deuteronomy 1:12, *New King James Version*).

Scripture: Deuteronomy 1:9-18
Song: "Just a Closer Walk with Thee"

Sadly, power plays are all too common in Christian fellowships. Some people want to be "in the spotlight" at any price. They don't like sharing the work; they become a one-man band.

Moses, in his dawning wisdom, eventually realized that God's work must be shared. As the Jewish nation grew, difficulties increased. Troubles multiplied and had to be sorted out. Growing populations always produce more problems, so Moses needed to find the best and wisest among the tribes to contribute their diplomatic skills for the benefit of the nation. Moses most certainly was not a loner at that point.

God's work is for sharing, and no one is to "lord it over" another. As seventeenth-century Bible commentator Matthew Henry said: "We must not grudge that God's work be done by other hands than ours, provided it be done by good hands."

And none of us is indispensable, of course, in spite of the reports! When it comes to God's work, it's crucial that we work well with others. Why? For the glory of God. But also in order to give all believers the blessed opportunity to exercise their spiritual gifts in kingdom service.

Thank You, **Father,** for giving me the ability to share. Help me to share Your work with others so they may also minister in Your church. Through Christ, amen.

February 3, 5–9. **David R. Nicholas** is a minister and writer who lives with his wife, Judith, in New South Wales, Australia. His interests are history, stamp-collecting, and photography.

Decide for Yourself

Nevertheless good things are found in you, in that you have removed the wooden images from the land, and have prepared your heart to seek God (2 Chronicles 19:3, New King James Version).

Scripture: 2 Chronicles 19:1-7
Song: "All to Jesus"

Brothers Christopher and Peter Hitchens had a similar up-bringing but took very different paths in life. Christopher was a member of the "New Atheists" who believed that the concept of a supreme being destroys individual freedom. In his book *God Is Not Great*, he wrote on atheism and the supposed negative effects of religion. Peter, on the other hand, became an active member of the Church of England. He advocates for moral virtues based on the Christian faith. His 2010 book, *The Rage Against God*, tells his own journey to faith and argues against the reasons that people use to reject God.

Father and son Asa and Jehoshaphat also took two very different approaches to faith in God. As king of Judah, Asa refused to seek God's will or obey His laws. Jehoshaphat was not a perfect king, but he did try to seek God's guidance and worked to remove idols from the land. Because he had "prepared [his] heart to seek God," the Lord blessed his reign.

Those who sincerely seek the true God will find him. We just need to prepare our hearts and head toward the Lord.

Father, thank You for offering us the freedom to make our own decisions to follow You. Give us hearts that are able to respond to Your call on our lives. In Jesus' name, amen.

February 4. **Cheryl J. Frey** is a professional proofreader living in Rochester, New York.

Justice and Mercy

Defend the poor and fatherless; Do justice to the afflicted and needy (Psalm 82:3, *New King James Version*).

Scripture: Psalm 82
Song: "Help Somebody Today"

Charles Spurgeon, the great English preacher of the 1800s, speaking on Psalm 82, told of Francis I of France. A woman knelt before him and begged for justice. The king said, "Justice I owe you, and justice you shall have. But if you *beg* anything of me, let it be mercy."

Our psalm tells us the poor and fatherless were at the mercy of judges. They were without money and without friends to help them. Such needed defending.

Times have changed but similar situations abound, as many still deal unkindly with the needy. The psalmist knew full well the need for mercy in human existence. While our verse calls for justice, we may also recall Micah 6:8, "What does the Lord require of you but to do justly, to love mercy, and to walk humbly with your God?"

Sometimes we miss opportunities to reach out and help others because we're so caught up with our own problems and difficulties. We have "I" trouble and fail to see those struggling right next to us. So today I'm asking the Lord to help me remember: when I help others I unwittingly help myself. I take one more step toward becoming a person characterized by a compassionate heart.

Gracious Lord, may I have the wisdom to extend mercy to those in need in my world. After all, how merciful You have been to me! In Jesus' name, amen.

Wealth and Wings

A man with an evil eye hastens after riches, And does not consider that poverty will come upon him (Proverbs 28:22, *New King James Version*).

Scripture: Proverbs 28:18-22
Song: "The Gift of Love"

A multimillionaire I knew fell sick and died. Then, of course, all his wealth was of little use to him. Further, after his death his family squabbled over what he had left behind. Even they found little comfort in riches.

Wealth comes; wealth goes. There's no certainty in it for, as the Bible says, "Riches certainly make themselves wings; they fly away like an eagle toward heaven" (Proverbs 23:5). Our verse provides a strong warning against the dangers that come with riches. Ironically, so often, some form of poverty tends to follow wealth.

Our western civilization is largely a consumer society, a sign of much riches. Yet personal debt is on the rise, and government spending seems to know no bounds. Nevertheless, a settled joy and happiness go undiscovered among the populace at large. No doubt the apostle James holds the key: "Every good gift and every perfect gift is from above, and comes down from the Father of lights" (1:17). When we recognize and understand this wonderful fact, we're able to keep riches in perspective and live for God's glory.

Dear Lord, I know that You are not so much concerned about how much money I give, but how much I consider to be purely my own. Remind me that all I have is on loan from You. Help me to be a good steward of Your riches! Through Christ, amen.

Judgment Is Coming

To Him all the prophets witness that, through His name, whoever believes in Him will receive remission of sins (Acts 10:43, *New King James Version*).

Scripture: Acts 10:34-43
Song: "Judge Me, O Lord, and Prove My Ways"

In the days of slavery in America, slaves would sing, "My Lord sees all you do, my Lord hears all you say, and my Lord keeps a writin' all the time." Such a song made plantation owners tremble, for it spoke of coming judgment. Indeed, the task of the Holy Spirit, down through the centuries, is to "convict the world of sin, and of righteousness, and of judgment" (John 16:8).

These days we hear little of judgment, so we do well to heed the words of Paul in Acts 10. Sin is our problem. Jesus, however, came into this world and dealt with that sin. When we enter the waters of baptism, we receive remission of our sins. Moreover, the Holy Spirit comes to dwell within us—and starts the lifelong process of making us holy (i.e., like Jesus). God has always had His witnesses and, all the while, He's creating new ones.

Isn't it wonderful to know that you are no longer separated from God, but rather joined to Him in Christ? Whenever we become aware of this great truth, we become strong ambassadors for Christ. Then when people look at us, they see Christ in us as their "hope of glory" (Colossians 1:27).

Thank You, **Almighty God and Father**, that Your Son has paid the price of all my sin. Now help me live a life of thanksgiving and praise until the day I stand before You with joy! In the precious name of Jesus my Savior. Amen.

Armored with the Word

The night is far spent, the day is at hand. Therefore let us cast off the works of darkness, and let us put on the armor of light (Romans 13:12, *New King James Version*).

Scripture: Romans 13:8-14
Song: "Labor On"

Lowell Mason's hymn arrangement puts it well, "Work, for the night is coming, work through the sunny noon; Fill brightest hours with labor, Rest comes sure and soon. Give every flying minute, something to keep in store."

Our verse today reflects a strong biblical theme that runs throughout the Scripture: the theme of darkness versus light, night versus day. And what a vast difference there is between the works of darkness and the works of light! So here's a firm challenge from the apostle Paul for us to throw off dark works and put on the armor of light, a call to change our way of living. The devil seeks to pull us down, but the Lord desires to build us up. The two ways are worlds apart and lead to very different places.

True love is the result of living in the light and walking in the light, even as Christ is the light of the world. It's night, but dawn is on the way. Therefore, we're wise when we use the armor God has provided—His Word. Will you join me in reading it today?

Father, today help me remember that the Christian walk means a constant conflict with the powers of darkness. I know that when I'm armed with Your Word, the works of darkness cannot harm me. You have given Your children the best—and ultimate—protection against all temptations. Thank You, through Christ my Lord. Amen.

No Favorites

If you show partiality, you commit sin, and are convicted by the law as transgressors (James 2:9, *New King James Version*).

Scripture: James 2:1-13
Song: "Earthly Pleasures Vainly Call Me"

When I lived in Melbourne, I discovered that the Nicholas family, makers of aspirin, were very wealthy (but I was not related). When I moved to Sydney, I began attending a Bible study there. A stranger approached me and said, "You're from Melbourne, so are you one of the Nicholas family?"

When I said, "No," he turned away and never spoke to me again, even though I saw him every week.

With ease we play favorites, an attitude to others that will quickly reveal our attitude to God. Here's what I mean: Show me how a person lives, and I'll tell you what they think of God.

Clearly, our text reminds us that we must not play favorites. It becomes easier to do if we'll stop and ask ourselves: *How can I compare the riches of Christ with the riches of this world?*

There is no comparison, yet we often give place to someone because they're rich in this world's goods. I want to remember today that I possess unsearchable riches in Christ (see Ephesians 3:8). True, the things of the world can bedazzle me at times. But they are so temporary, and the face of Christ, my Lord, shines so much more brightly, even than gold. He it is who will fill my vision throughout eternity.

Heavenly Father, help me see everyone as equal in Your sight. Remind me that, at the foot of the cross, the ground is completely level! In Jesus' name, amen.

Increasing Faith

We ought always to thank God for you . . . because your faith is growing more and more, and the love all of you have for one another is increasing (2 Thessalonians 1:3).

Scripture: 2 Thessalonians 1:3-12
Song: "Growing Dearer Each Day"

I am an online missionary, inviting people to know more of Christ through the Internet. About six months ago, Mike wrote in and committed his life to the Lord. I answer dozens of e-mails from people like him who have expressed faith in Jesus Christ, but Mike's story touched me.

Mike is paralyzed. When he first contacted me, Mike asked questions about why he was paralyzed, wondering whether God loved him. Over several months, I shared my faith and helped him realize that having a disability isn't the end of the world. My friend was eventually baptized. And he sometimes says: "I can see how my disability is actually a gift."

Today's verse encourages me. Not only am I blessed to minister to folks like Mike, but my faith and love increase as I do so. I learn more about the Lord when I research a question, and my prayer life deepens as I intercede for a new believer.

What are you doing today to increase your faith and deepen your prayer life? Could you send an encouraging Scripture to a friend or pray for the person in front of you at the store?

Lord, help me find new ways to increase my faith and show my love today. May I be creative in the ways I do it. In the name of Jesus, amen.

February 10–16. **Tait Berge**, living in Colorado Springs, is the Church Relations Director at Mephibosheth Ministry. When not working, he enjoys sports, especially hockey and golf.

Want to Be Skillful for Christ?

Fight the good fight of the faith. Take hold of the eternal life to which you were called when you made your good confession in the presence of many witnesses (1 Timothy 6:12).

Scripture: 1 Timothy 6:6-12
Song: "Weary, Burdened Wanderer"

I'm tired. My body aches. I don't want to do this anymore. *I quit, Lord!*

That has been my attitude for the last couple of weeks. The Lord feels far away. The words aren't coming out for my writing projects, and typing with bad hands and shoulders is painful at best. I wonder if anyone I've ministered to recently really accepts the message of the good news of God's love. Bottom line: Does my work in the kingdom of God really matter?

Then I read today's verse, and I remember—the last time I felt near the Lord, the last time I received positive feedback on my writing, and an encouraging note from someone I've discipled. Most of all, I remember the time when I first said "yes" to Christ's call to ministry.

Today's verse is a good reminder for me as I battle my discouragement. I must remember to fight the good fight of my faith. How about you? Will you join me in fighting the good fight of faith in times of discouragement? Our times of spiritual dryness and all our adversities are working to make us stronger. As one African proverb puts it: "Smooth seas do not make skillful sailors."

Father, help me to battle my discouragement and to fight the good fight of faith, no matter the circumstances. You are sufficient in all things! Through Christ, amen.

The Power of Prayer

May the Lord make your love increase and overflow for each other and for everyone else, just as ours does for you (1 Thessalonians 3:12).

Scripture: 1 Thessalonians 3:4-13
Song: "Let Us Love and Sing and Wonder"

Sometimes I don't know where to begin to pray. I stumble on words, and names refuse to come to mind.

The other day, sitting in worship, I started to pray for everyone that came to mind. I prayed for the worship leader. I prayed for my brother's family, and I lifted my brother before the Lord, that he might receive the good news and become a Christian. I also prayed for my mom and my fiancée.

I looked up when I finished. I couldn't believe where the time had gone.

My brothers live in other states, and I haven't seen them for a long time, yet my prayers for them helped me realize how much God is concerned for them. My prayers for my mother's health helped me realize that she is God's child too. When I prayed for my fiancée, I realized in a deeper way how much she means to me.

My love for the people I prayed for increased that day. Each person is close to me, and I saw each of them through the Lord's eyes. I am newly aware of the power of prayer. Our love increases as we pray for everyone on our prayer lists.

Lord, I want to pray more during my days! Help me to see that this is never time wasted, but that it is at the heart of Your will for me. So, increase my love as I pray for my family, my friends, strangers, and even my enemies. Through Christ, amen.

Why Not?

When Jesus heard this, he was amazed at him, and turning to the crowd following him, he said, "I tell you, I have not found such great faith even in Israel" (Luke 7:9).

Scripture: Luke 7:1-10
Song: "Faith Is a Living Power from Heaven"

Have you ever thought about amazing Jesus? Is it even possible? After all, Jesus is all-powerful and all-knowing, the Alpha and Omega . . . the very Son of God.

According to Scripture, a certain man amazed our Lord. It was a Gentile, a commander in the Roman army, and his servant was sick. But he came to a Jewish rabbi, believing this humble preacher could heal his servant. In the commander's view, Jesus wouldn't even need to come to the place where the sick one lay. Just saying a few words would suffice; healing would follow.

What faith! Luke tells us that Jesus was amazed. Was it because the soldier was a Roman—yet still believed? Was it because the entire religious culture of the day would naturally deny such a possibility? (After all, some of the religious folks thought Jesus' healings were actually from the devil!)

Let us learn from this soldier's outlook on the miraculous. Do we believe Jesus still heals? I know that I would like to amaze Jesus with a powerful depth of faith—that He might accomplish marvelous things in and through me as I seek to do His will. Today I may even ask Jesus to do something impossible, something only He could do. Why not?

Lord, give me the boldness to ask for the impossible from You. Give me the insight, as well, to make sure it conforms to Your kingdom plans! In Jesus' name, amen.

Valentine for Jesus

As she stood behind him at his feet weeping, she began to wet his feet with her tears. Then she wiped them with her hair, kissed them and poured perfume on them (Luke 7:38).

Scripture: Luke 7:36-50
Song: "Merciful Savior, Come and Be My Comfort"

Today is Valentine's Day, a day when we show "sweet" love to the special people in our lives. Typically we give cards or chocolate, but sometimes our gifts are more extravagant—like perfume. Jesus received a jar of perfume one day, and it changed a woman's life.

We know the story well. Jesus is dining at Simon's house when a woman starts kissing His feet and wiping them with her hair. She pours perfume on them.

This is a beautiful scene, marred only by one sad fact: Everyone knew who this woman was—a prostitute. But outweighing everything is this happy, blessed fact: Jesus showed mercy, extended compassion, forgave her sins.

Isn't it interesting that the woman gave her gift *before* Jesus forgave her? She took a risk in extending herself, letting down and being vulnerable. With this opening of her heart lay the chance that she might be severely scolded and sent away—or worse.

What can you and I give to Jesus on this Valentine's Day? The same thing this woman gave: an open, sweet heart.

Heavenly Father, on this Valentine Day, I give You my best gift: willingly, I give You my whole self. And thank You for Your greater gift to me—forgiveness and unconditional love through the merits of Your Son, in whom I pray. Amen.

Don't Compare

So then, just as you received Christ Jesus as Lord, continue to live your lives in him, rooted and built up in him, strengthened in the faith as you were taught, and overflowing with thankfulness (Colossians 2:6, 7).

Scripture: Colossians 2:1-7
Song: "Ten Thousand Thanks to Jesus"

Lately I've felt that my ministry borders on the meaningless. I sit down to hammer out a devotional or two or write an encouraging e-mail to a friend, and I wonder if my effort is worth it. *Do my words mean anything? Am I making any difference in people's lives?*

To make matters worse, I came across a story about someone who is—clearly, and obvious to all—making a real difference. This person is speaking, traveling, and writing books. People follow her on twitter. Compared to my small ministry, it seems the Lord is using her so much more than He is using me.

Today's verse helps me reverse my thinking. I've received Christ as my Lord and accepted His calling on my life. I have been built up in Christ. I am being strengthened in my faith. Instead of envying another's ministry, perhaps I could use this verse as an encouragement to renew my thinking—and approach each new day of work with the joy of the Lord. Yes, this verse helps me understand that my calling is unique to me. So why should I ever compare myself to others?

Almighty and most merciful God, each day help me live in the truth that Your calling is designed especially and uniquely for each of Your servants. Forgive my jealousy toward the ministries of other brothers and sisters in the body of Christ. Help me to be grateful for all that You pour into my life. In the name of Jesus, amen.

Why Hold Anything Back?

Was not our father Abraham considered righteous for what he did when he offered his son Isaac on the altar? . . . His faith was made complete by what he did (James 2:21, 22).

Scripture: James 2:14-26
Song: "Faith of Our Fathers"

My faith was tested when I met a woman with whom I envisioned spending the rest of my life. Before we could marry, however, we discovered obstacles in our way. We both used wheelchairs and needed a big enough place to live. Our finances wouldn't meet our needs, and friends warned me to be careful.

Still, I was convinced that God would provide for us, and I went forward, planning a new life with my fiancée. I did everything to try and make this work—including being willing to give up everything I had.

As I think back to that time, I rejoice in the many ways my faith grew amidst my increasing willingness to obey the Lord. He may have indeed asked me to marry, but he eventually pulled me back from giving up everything. Like Abraham, I believe that God tested my love for Him, bringing me to the brink of making life-changing decisions.

Is God asking you to do something difficult? Do you love Him enough to give it all up? Remember that His "tests" are always for the purpose of displaying our genuine faith. As the severely tested Job proclaimed: "He knows the way that I take; when he has tested me, I will come forth as gold" (Job 23:10).

Lord, amidst my trials, help me remember to ask: "How will He use this to grow my faith?" In other words, help me turn my faith into action! In Jesus' name, amen.

Already There

"Because the poor are plundered and the needy groan, I will now arise," says the LORD. "I will protect them" (Psalm 12:5).

Scripture: Psalm 12
Song: "Rescue the Perishing"

A few years ago, I took a group of teenagers on a mission trip to Juarez, Mexico. In the months leading up to the trip, our team met together on a regular basis for training and preparation. After a few sessions, I realized that team members seemed to have a skewed perspective on the importance of our ministry to the Mexican people. I sensed a subtle arrogance, for example, about how we were going to take the hope of Jesus to "those poor, suffering people."

As I prayed during the next week, I began to realize that these people weren't just sitting around waiting on us to come to them! The Lord showed me that they were not without hope. He also convinced me that we were not taking Jesus to Mexico—because He was already there among the poor. We were simply going to *join Him in His work,* in order to win the hearts of those He already deeply loved.

Here in this psalm, God declares that He will arise and protect the weak and needy. Wherever we find poverty and suffering, there we will find God.

Heavenly Father, You are there in the midst of humanity's pain, just as You were centuries ago, when Jesus took on flesh and dwelt among us. In His name, amen.

February 17–23. **Mark Williams** is an associate minister, college professor, and freelance writer who lives with his wife, Kelley, and their seven children near Nashville, Tennessee.

Victory in the Valley

The Philistines occupied one hill and the Israelites another, with the valley between them (1 Samuel 17:3).

Scripture: 1 Samuel 17:1-11
Song: "How Great Is Our God"

As a child I played basketball each year in a league run by the local YMCA. My older brother was the undisputed star of the team, while I kept the bench warm for him during the games.

At the end of one season, our team had progressed to the championship game, and the score was very close as we headed to the end of the fourth quarter. The game was exciting, friends and family were cheering, and my stomach was in knots.

At a decisive point—in the final seconds—one of our players fouled out. As the coach turned toward our bench, I heard my voice say, "Please don't put me in, Coach." I was afraid I'd make a mistake and be the reason our team lost the game.

Ouch. Today, I am still embarrassed at my cowardice in that moment. All the glory and excitement were out on that floor, but I settled for the view from the bench on the sidelines.

As Goliath came out from his camp each morning, the Israelites watched from the sidelines as well. Fear and discouragement ran through their ranks as he shouted out his threats each day. The victory was there for the taking, but the Israelite army just sat on the bench.

O God my Father, today give me the courage to get off the sidelines and find victory in the valley with You! Help me to remember that You and I, working for the advance of Your kingdom, are always an overwhelming offensive threat! In the name of Jesus, who lives and reigns with You and the Holy Spirit, amen.

Just One Sacrifice

At that time they sacrificed to the LORD seven hundred head of cattle and seven thousand sheep and goats from the plunder they had brought back (2 Chronicles 15:11).

Scripture: 2 Chronicles 15:1-12
Song: "Nothing but the Blood"

I once helped an elderly relative with two different eyedrops: one went in the left eye four times a day and the other in both eyes three times a day—but not at the same time as the other drops. How I wished there were drops that worked with just one dose a day!

In the Old Testament, the sacrificial system was also complicated. It demanded that different animals be sacrificed for the forgiveness of the sins of the people. In this passage, thousands of animals were slaughtered as an atoning sacrifice.

Can you imagine how long it would take to slaughter 7,000 sheep and goats or 700 head of cattle? Can you see the river of blood that would flow from the altar as the throats were slit? Can you smell the stench of death, see the pile of carcasses? It would be hard to stomach . . . so much blood . . . constantly repeated.

Yet, on the cross, we find an eternally effective bloodletting, putting an end to the old way. As the writer of Hebrews put it: "It is impossible for the blood of bulls and goats to take away sins. Therefore . . . we have been made holy through the sacrifice of the body of Jesus Christ once for all" (10:4, 5, 10).

Dear Father in Heaven, I rejoice and give thanks for the perfect lamb of God, the once-for-all sacrifice for sin. In His victory over death, I am victorious in life. Help me to remember His cross today and live in His power. Through Jesus' name, amen.

Hearing When He Speaks

When I heard these things, I sat down and wept. For some days I mourned and fasted and prayed (Nehemiah 1:4).

Scripture: Nehemiah 1
Song: "Sweet Hour of Prayer"

Back in my early days of ministry, I served as a youth minister for a larger church in eastern Tennessee. One year, as high school graduation approached, I was asked if I would like to preach in our main services on the Sunday morning that we honored our high school graduates. As I had never preached in a Sunday morning service before, I was both excited and terrified.

Even though I was nervous, I sensed the presence of the Holy Spirit with me as I prayed for inspiration in my preaching. I was reminded of how Nehemiah fasted and prayed when he heard about the condition of his people, and I sensed that God was calling me to fast and pray as well.

I started my fast on Monday morning and felt that God was calling me to fast for five days. Each day, I read the Scriptures and prayed for His guidance. Slowly, as the week progressed, the sermon God had planned for me became clear. When I stepped to that pulpit on Sunday morning, I was confident that God had a message for our graduates and their families. That sermon, "Advice for the Ages," is still tucked away in my files in my office . . . as a reminder that God speaks when I listen.

Almighty and everlasting God, when I face tough decisions or need a word from You, remind me that You will speak when I seek You with prayer and fasting. In the name of Jesus, Lord and Savior of all, I pray. Amen.

A Need . . . or a Greed?

Before I finished praying in my heart, Rebekah came out, with her jar on her shoulder. She went down to the spring and drew water, and I said to her, "Please give me a drink" (Genesis 24:45).

Scripture: Genesis 24:42-52
Song: "God Is Able"

I dread taking my younger children to the grocery store because of the checkout aisle. Our shopping usually goes fairly well until we come to this treasure trove of goodies, all exactly positioned at eye level in a child's world. It's here that they start begging me to buy something for them. "Daddy, can I please get some candy? *Please?*" Sometimes I give in (especially to my 3-year-old daughter) and let them each pick one thing. At other times, with more resolve, I refuse.

Either way, it's a good teachable moment where I remind them that they don't actually *need* what they are asking for, they simply *want* it. I am standing with a basketful of needs: milk, bread, fruit, cereal . . . to carry us through the week.

God in His generosity has always provided for our family. He is faithful to take care of our needs, both spiritually and physically, but not always as quick to give us our wants on demand.

As in our Scripture passage, God is working to provide our needs before the prayer passes our lips. Why? Because these things are in His will for us and are good for our growth and development.

O Lord God, thank You for providing all of my needs according to Your will for me. Help me also to want the things You want for me. In Jesus' name, amen.

It's All in the Name

The name of the LORD is a fortified tower; the righteous run to it and are safe (Proverbs 18:10).

Scripture: Proverbs 18:2-13
Song: "Blessed Be Your Name"

Part of good marketing is to sell not only your product but also your name. Companies spend millions each year trying to help us remember their brand and become loyal customers of that name. For example, as I was growing up, my father always encouraged me to buy a certain brand of appliance "because the name meant quality." Now, as an adult, I have a tendency to look for this product because I've come to believe it's higher quality, based entirely on the name.

The ancient Israelites knew God by a special name. When we see the word *LORD* capitalized in Scripture, it refers to the Hebrew name *Jehovah*. This name was, and is, so holy among Jews that many won't say it aloud even today. (They say *Adonai* in its place.)

Instead of being known by an image or a form, the God of Israel chose to be known by His name. And this name is more than just some letters across the front of a shirt; it is pregnant with meaning. This name means love, faithfulness, and strength. It means that God is a refuge in a time of trouble. He is our redemption. He is the LORD, and we are His people walking together with Him.

Lord, today may I truly come to understand that You alone are my refuge and strength. With each problem I face in the days ahead, remind me that I can trust in You to carry me through. In Jesus' name, amen.

Sticks and Stones

Out of the same mouth come praise and cursing. My brothers and sisters, this should not be (James 3:10).

Scripture: James 3:1-12
Song: "They'll Know We Are Christians by Our Love"

"Sticks and stones may break my bones, but words can never hurt me!" As children, we chanted this rhyme at recess to other children who were being mean or making fun of us. As a young child, I took it at face value; as an adult, I believe it to be an unadulterated lie.

In reality, it has been my experience that sticks and stones can *only* break your bones, while words can damage and scar your heart for a lifetime. Broken bones heal in a matter of months; broken hearts sometimes never heal.

Having worked in church ministry for over 20 years, I am amazed by the number of people who carry deep wounds because of things that were said to them by their parents, spouses, children, friends, or fellow church members. These memories can affect a person's self worth, their view of God, and their ability to love others.

The tongue can be a "fire" and a "world of evil," but it can also be something much more powerful. Words of love and forgiveness can save a marriage; words of compassion can heal a friendship; words of praise and encouragement can lift the spirits of a child. As followers of Christ, our words should reflect the love we have for one another.

Holy Spirit, fill my mouth today with words that build others up and bring You glory! In the name of Jesus, my Savior, I pray. Amen.

Stronger Than the Surf

Your statutes, LORD, stand firm; holiness adorns your house for endless days (Psalm 93:5).

Scripture: Psalm 93
Song: "He Wills That I Should Holy Be"

Living in the corner of Kansas, our trips to the ocean are rare. So it was with tremendous anticipation that my wife and I visited the coast of northern Oregon some years ago. Its rugged, rocky beauty did not disappoint us!

As we stood on the rocks, it was impossible not to feel some sense of awe as the waves crashed in, again and again and again. How could anything withstand such power? Surely, in another ten thousand years, every block and boulder would be ground to sand. The constant pounding of the waves and the wind could eventually send even the hardest rock into the beach. And yet, the coastline still holds, the beaches still stand. The ocean is still held in check.

Of how much greater power is the Word of God! Through the centuries it has withstood the bitterest attacks. Even though the enemies of truth still seek to silence the Scriptures, the revelation of the Lord through His prophets and apostles, through the Son himself, still guides, still stands firm. Against the relentless attacks of the enemy, the statutes of the Lord provide us with a solid anchor for life and for living.

O God, though the winds of life beat against me, sustain me by the power of Your Word. Let my feet be firmly anchored on the truth of Christ. In His name, amen.

February 24–28. **Doc Arnett** is the director of Institutional Research at Highland Community College and minister of New Life Church in Blair, Kansas.

A Sure Refuge

Kiss his son, or he will be angry and your way will lead to your destruction, for his wrath can flare up in a moment. Blessed are all who take refuge in him (Psalm 2:12).

Scripture: Psalm 2
Song: "Rest in Jesus"

My wife and I live in an old farmhouse in northeastern Kansas. Our gravel driveway runs straight up from the highway to our backdoor. Down near the road, just at the end of the small horse paddock, was an old evergreen shrub. Over the years it had spread out to nearly 20 feet wide. Many of the branches had died and turned brown and ugly. So I decided to get rid of it.

As I'd hoped, my little utility tractor with its hydraulic bucket loader made short work of the project. As I raised the tangled mass of roots and branches up from the ground, I saw a rabbit shoot out from underneath, streaking toward the tree line a few hundred feet away. The cottontail had held to its hiding place throughout the upheavals of the tractor's work. I chuckled as I imagined the rabbit's astonishment as its dense, sheltering cover had been plucked up into the sky!

When we take refuge in the Son of God, we do not have to worry that one day our true shelter will be destroyed. There is no force on Heaven or earth that can overcome Him who protects us. While all else might be shaken and removed, those who hide their souls in Him need never fear.

I thank You, **Lord,** and give You praise, that You have provided me with the refuge of Your arms. Keep me safe, I pray, in the name of Jesus. Amen.

The Right Blend

In your majesty ride forth victoriously in the cause of truth, humility and justice; let your right hand achieve awesome deeds (Psalm 45:4).

Scripture: Psalm 45:1-9
Song: "Majesty"

Although my cooking experiments usually turn out to be edible, they don't always turn out to be desirable. One reason is that I'm not at all reluctant to substitute and experiment.

Recently, I wanted to make some cookies. Since we didn't have any graham cracker crumbs on hand, I substituted some crushed cinnamon squares cereal. Dark brown molasses filled in for light corn syrup. Seems like there was another substitution or two as well. Anyway . . . to make a short story shorter, the experiment was less than amazingly successful. Too many strong flavors competing for limited taste capacity, I suppose.

Just as we need balance in our favorite recipes, we need balance in our battles for hearts and souls. So often, we see people on different sides of some issue rip one another apart like piranhas in a feeding frenzy. When we're so convinced of the justice of our cause and the truth of our claims that we forget humility, we depart from the example and spirit of Christ.

I remember something I heard an old preacher say years ago: "Christianity doesn't make someone mean." If even the cause of Christ should be pursued by "speaking the truth in love," shouldn't all of our lesser causes also be pursued in humility?

Dear Lord in Heaven, help me to remain humble, even when fighting for truth and justice. I pray through my deliverer, Jesus. Amen.

Righteous Judgment

Judgment will again be founded on righteousness, and all the upright in heart will follow it (Psalm 94:15).

Scripture: Psalm 94:8-15
Song: "Judge Eternal, Throned in Splendor"

As an administrator and teacher at a small community college, I sometimes have the opportunity to do some informal counseling. Recently, a young man sat in my office and poured out his heart. "I think I'm cursed," he confided. With little prompting, he shared some of the episodes from his young life.

After a while, I started to probe a little bit, asking him for details of one thing and another. Soon, I was able to show the young man that in every one of these episodes, he'd demonstrated a pattern of making decisions without getting the required information — or just ignoring the available information.

I've found, in my own life, and seen frequently in the lives of others, that most of the blame for bad situations rests ultimately on the decisions that we have made for ourselves. Either we use a faulty foundation or we ignore truth and righteousness. That's when we begin paying a high price for our bad choices.

I suppose it seems easier to blame God for the messes we find ourselves in — or to chalk it up to "being cursed" (or just having a run of bad luck). It's easier than to accept that responsibility ourselves. But to choose and use righteousness as the foundation of our decisions brings life and blessing.

Dear Lord, help us all, whether young or old, to make righteousness the bedrock of our judgments. Before taking important steps may I immerse the decision in prayer and get the information I need. In Jesus' name, amen.

The Applause of Earth

Let the rivers clap their hands, let the mountains sing together for joy (Psalm 98:8).

Scripture: Psalm 98
Song: "Come, O Creator Spirit Blest"

I have been fascinated by water since I was a little kid. Whether wading in the tiny creek that ran through the woods on our Kentucky farm or standing on an ocean beach, I have always been captivated. Because of their beauty, power, and sparkling reflections, the waters of the world draw me to contemplation, admiration, and appreciation for our maker.

The rivers are my favorites, especially the rock-bed streams of the mountain regions. I love the feel of cold, smooth stone against my feet as I wade cautiously. I love the smell and feel of the spray at the base of a waterfall. Whether running the rapids in a canoe or just sitting on a huge boulder and feeling the fall sun on my face, I love the experience.

It is easy in the surging sounds of the waterfall and the rapids to sense that the rivers are, indeed, clapping their hands. For the believer, the thunderous applause becomes an expression of admiration for the creator.

Yes, the rushing waters of the earth applaud Heaven for the joy of their being. So how much more fitting it is for us to shout for the joy of our salvation.

O God, Creator of Heaven and earth, with all of my being, I applaud You for the beauty of Your creation and for the joy of the salvation You have given the world through Christ Jesus. When I look at the glories of this universe, let me lift my voice to You in praise. Through Christ my precious Lord, amen.

My Prayer Notes

My Prayer Notes

_____

_____

_____

_____

_____

_____

_____

_____

_____

_____

_____

_____

_____

_____

_____

_____

_____

_____

_____

_____

_____

_____

_____

My Prayer Notes